Coaching for Wellbeing

Coaching for Wellbeing

An Evidence-Based Guide for Practitioners

Ana Paula Nacif

Mc Graw Hill   Open University Press

Open University Press
McGraw Hill
Unit 4,
Foundation Park
Roxborough Way
Maidenhead
SL6 3UD

email: emea_uk_ireland@mheducation.com
world wide web: www.openup.co.uk

First edition published 2023

A catalogue record of this book is available from the British Library

ISBN-13: 9780335251902
ISBN-10: 0335251900
eISBN: 9780335251919

Library of Congress Cataloging-in-Publication Data
CIP data applied for

Typeset by Transforma Pvt. Ltd., Chennai, India

Praise page

"This intensely practical book offers a cutting-edge, evidence-based framework for coaches and other helping professionals seeking to more effectively address the need to promote wellbeing in times of increasing mental distress. It is the first book of its type to bridge contemporary wellbeing concepts and theories with one-to-one and group coaching. Ana Nacif's expertise shines through, providing illuminating case studies and a comprehensive roadmap for coaching for wellbeing based on research and years of experience in the field. Highly recommended."

Dr Andrea Giraldez-Hayes, Director of the Wellbeing and Psychological Services Centre and Programme Director, Masters in Positive Psychology and Coaching Psychology, University of East London, UK

"Coaching for wellbeing will become essential for positive psychology, health and wellbeing coaches everywhere. Ana Paula Nacif brings a light touch to complex topics, making them understandable and accessible. She has skilfully combined theory and research with a practical focus – from PERMA and BeWell models to three good things and gratitude letters – making this book the perfect place to start a journey of discovery in bringing evidenced-based psychology into your coaching practice."

Professor Jonathan Passmore, Henley Business School & EZRA Coaching, UK

"While wellbeing is a highly sought-after state, its broad nature can leave many coaches uncertain about where to begin or how to direct their coaching efforts.

This book effectively transforms the abstract concept of well-being into tangible, applicable know-how. Using a dynamic combination of models, diagrams, case studies, imaginative exercises and practical wisdom, it serves as an engaging guide on your journey towards understanding wellbeing and having an idea of how to tackle it in your work. Happy reading!"

Professor Ilona Boniwell, CEO of Positran, France, and Programme Director and Course Leader at UEL, UK

"The relevance of the idea of wellbeing for everyone is unquestionable, but this notion is far from simple. Ana Paula Nacif describes wellbeing as a complex and multi-faceted concept and, from this position, invites the reader to explore the multiple ways in which wellbeing can *be conceptualised and what it is like to support people towards a state that is so valuable but difficult to pin down. The book represents a good balance of theory and ideas for practice for a curious practitioner and will be a very useful read."*

Professor Tatiana Bachkirova, Professor of Coaching
Psychology at Oxford Brookes University, UK

Contents

List of Figures

List of Tables

Acknowledgements

First and foremost, this book would not have been possible without all my amazing coaching clients. Your humanity, your strength, your vulnerability, and your commitment to life and being well, even under the most challenging circumstances, made me want to delve deeper into this elusive and fluid concept we call wellbeing. You are the greatest source of inspiration for my professional and academic life and, for that, I am forever grateful. Your life stories helped me make sense of the theories and practices I share in this book. You also showed me the true meaning of this quote, often attributed to Carl Jung: 'Know all the theories, master all the techniques, but as you touch a human soul, be just another human soul.'

Thank you to the organisations, and of course the great people working in them, who are committed to fostering wellbeing, who have welcomed me and my ideas, and are willing to learn together.

This book would not have been possible without the academic team at Oxford Brookes University, where I completed my doctoral studies. Thank you to my supervisors Ioanna Iordanou and Judie Gannon for their endless patience and guidance. I am also grateful to Tatiana Bachkirova and Elaine Cox who have inspired me to challenge my own thinking and look at things from different perspectives.

I would also like to thank the amazing people in my team at the University of East London: Andrea Giraldez-Hayes, Ilona Boniwell, Hanna Kampman, Ayse Burcin Baskurt, Candan Ertubey, Laura Martin, Lucy Ryan and Mette Marie Ledertoug. I am also grateful to my students, whose enthusiasm and commitment inspire and energise me.

I'm grateful to the team at the Open University Press, for believing in this project, for encouraging me to keep going when I was not sure I could, and for making this book happen.

A special thank you goes to Christian van Nieuwerburgh, for his invaluable guidance and generosity over many years.

Last, but by no means least, a huge thanks goes to my husband Anthony, my daughter Gabriela, and my son Daniel, for their love and support.

Introduction

Western society is changing, in paradoxical ways. On one hand, over the past decades, the narrative of performance in the workplace has been slowly replaced by that of professional development and more humane practices, including a concern for employees' wellbeing. There has been a clear drive to reduce the stigma around mental illness and a willingness to talk more openly about feelings. On the other hand, workload demand on employees seems to be ever increasing; in many sectors such as health, social care and education, to name just a few, people are constantly asked to do more with fewer resources and less time. Stress and mental distress have become regular features of the workplace.

About 15 years ago, after completing my coaching qualification, I stumbled upon wellbeing, as a focus for coaching, when I started working with organisations supporting people in communities. At that time, the focus seemed to be on 'happiness' and people's life satisfaction as preferred ways to think about the idea of people being well and feeling good. The question in people's minds seemed to be: *how can we be happier?* Even the UK government launched its own *Happiness Index* in 2010 in an attempt to understand how people's lives are improving not only by measuring standards of living (as reflected in the country's GDP), but also by asking people about their perceived quality of life. Since then, there has been a shift from single measures, such as happiness or life satisfaction, to multi-dimensional approaches, which are more holistic. This shift has also been reflected in our everyday language and society, with the word wellbeing becoming embedded in the narrative of everyday life.

In my work with organisations, I noticed the shift from a 'coaching for performance' approach to coaching as a tool for professional development and growth. And, while working in organisations to support people's growth and professional development, it became apparent to me that some of the issues clients were bringing to coaching were linked to their wellbeing. They were grappling with managing their professional and personal lives and the impact of their choices on their physical and mental health. Some of my clients were at risk of burnout and were dissatisfied with their lives – from women executives finding it impossible to reconcile their professional aspirations with their family lives, to frontline social care workers feeling completely exhausted and defeated by impossible work conditions. Wellbeing became a topic of interest for me, and I started to explore with my clients how 'being well' could lay the foundation for change in other areas of their lives.

The multi-faceted nature of wellbeing means that each client's experience is unique. In my work in communities, I noticed how my personal views of wellbeing were biased and limited to my views of the world and upbringing. My clients taught me to look at wellbeing from a myriad of perspectives. For example, I remember being humbled by a client who explained to me why he continued to smoke heavily, despite knowing this was bad for his health. (He was in his sixties and lived with multiple long-term health conditions.) He proudly declared being sober for three years and having just managed to secure a volunteer position at a local charity. With a cheeky smile on his face, he said, 'You can't win them all, Ana!' Another client, a young woman, told me about how her family did not support her attempt to go back into education, and how that made her feel 'really bad'. They felt that she had a reasonably good job and that 'education was not for her' as they didn't have the means to support her financially. She felt something was missing. She did well at school and wanted an intellectual challenge. She knew she could do it and wanted to prove herself. And that's what moved her, whereas staying where she was – even though her family felt it was safe – was having a negative impact on how she felt about herself and her life.

As my clients presented their personal stories and challenges, I sought to build a better understanding of different coaching models, tools and theories to support them. It was a daunting task, as I felt like I was going from pillar to post, with umpteen options and directions for my professional learning and development. As the coaching field also developed and more research started to emerge, I wanted to ensure that my practice was robust and based on sound theoretical underpinnings and evidence. I noticed that not only was there a lack of research into coaching for wellbeing, but also that the available resources, which were specifically developed for coaches wanting to work in this area, were limited.

I decided to embark upon a professional doctorate to research coaching for wellbeing to expand my understanding of this exciting field of human experience. In this book, I share some of the learning that emerged from the research, alongside the practical experience of working with clients from all walks of life over several years.

This is the book that I wish had been available to me when I started to develop my practice in coaching for wellbeing. It is aimed at coaches and other professionals who are interested in learning more about evidence-based practice in this field. The book provides an overview of the key theories of wellbeing, research and practice to support you and your clients in their wellbeing adventure.

Wellbeing is a fascinating area of work, and it is a vast multi-disciplinary field, which cannot be contained in one book. I hope the ideas I share will inspire you to continue to learn and challenge your thinking in this rewarding field of coaching practice.

The structure of the book

Part I discusses wellbeing paradigms and theories. I explore different perspectives and definitions of wellbeing and how these inform and impact our coaching practice. This section of the book explains some core wellbeing theories, such as psychological wellbeing, positive psychology, self-determination theory, and flow.

Part II focuses on bringing theories and paradigms to life. It takes you through the applied practice of the theories explored in Part I. It shows how the theory informs the coaching practice and it includes practical tools and techniques that can be used with individual coaching clients as well as when working with organisations. This section of the book includes theories about sustainable change, the role of motivation and practical suggestions to help clients achieve long-lasting changes. Lastly, I explore the boundaries of coaching and ethical considerations. I invite you to consider issues around mental health and wellbeing, and the questions they raise regarding the limitations of coaching for wellbeing practices.

In Part III, I showcase the BeWell Coaching for Wellbeing model and its application. This evidence-based model was developed through empirical research and brings together some of the theories and paradigms discussed throughout the book. Part III briefly revisits a few theoretical concepts, and explains step-by-step how the model can be used in practice. I also explore the benefits of delivering the model in group interventions, including some of the key considerations for practitioners wanting to work in groups in organisations and other settings, such as schools, community groups and health.

In various chapters of this book, I share case studies and anecdotal evidence from my coaching practice. These examples have been chosen to illustrate the applications of coaching for wellbeing, as well as some of the challenges. The individual examples are based on real clients whose names and contexts have been changed to protect their identities. I also include examples of organisations committed to this type of work in the corporate and not-for-profit sectors to give you a flavour of the work that is currently being undertaken and to invite you and others to consider what else can be done to take coaching for wellbeing to more people who can benefit from it.

At the end of the book, I provide an Appendix, a toolkit for coaches, which includes a set of basic coaching for wellbeing tools and exercises to support your coaching practice. Last, but by no means least, it is important to remind ourselves that wellbeing must always be considered within a systemic context. While individuals may be able to take steps to improve their wellbeing, social determinants of health, as proposed by the World Health Organization, are equally important. These include education, income, job security, working life conditions, food insecurity, housing, and social inclusion. As such, coaches need to consider the ethical and social impact of their practice.

There will be some challenges on the way, but this is amazing and rewarding work. Enjoy!

Part **1**

Wellbeing concept and theories

1   Wellbeing paradigms and definitions

The wellbeing landscape

Wellbeing has become a topic of great significance and interest to individuals, organisations, and society in general. There is a wide recognition that 'being well' is important for all of us, and that our wellbeing has a tangible impact on the various aspects of our lives. It has been associated with improvements in physical health and longevity (Boehm & Kubzansky, 2012; Hill & Turiano, 2014; Pressman & Cohen, 2005). It has a positive impact on relationships (Lyubomirsky et al., 2005). People with high levels of wellbeing are more likely to contribute to their communities (Isen & Levin, 1972). In the workplace, wellbeing has been associated with better work productivity (Lyubomirsky et al., 2005) and there is a widespread recognition that health and wellbeing are crucial for the long-term success of any business. Because of its importance, wellbeing is a popular topic of discussion in many spheres of life, including politics, economics, social care, health and organisational development.

Yet, our individual and collective journeys to wellbeing are not always straightforward. Habits of a lifetime, unhelpful personal and societal narratives, and our very fallible human nature can make the pursuit of wellbeing rewarding and frustrating in equal measure.

Coaching, as a practice that supports people to reflect on their lives and to make positive changes, is well placed to help clients along the way. This is an incredibly rewarding field of coaching – one that puts us at the heart of what matters to our clients, and which creates the foundation for them to pursue their dreams and aspirations. It enables them to create better lives, or to help them cope with gruelling life circumstances. Although social media posts would have us believe that wellbeing comes with a fair share of calm oceans, inspiring landscapes and perfectly balanced life, real life tends to be somewhat more turbulent. As we and our clients grapple with our daily experiences of well*being*, coaching becomes less about *doing* and more about *being*, and about leveraging *being* to achieve the desired changes. One of the crucial characteristics of coaching for wellbeing is the fact that wellbeing is all-encompassing and touches upon many areas of our lives. As such, it does not lend itself to neat goals that can be achieved in a particular timeframe and ticked off our list. We can't do wellbeing on a Monday and be done with it for the day, week, month, or year. Like that gym membership that does not make us fitter unless we show up, coaching for wellbeing can only go so far. As we collaborate with our clients, we aim to help them understand themselves better and consider their daily choices and the impact these have on their wellbeing. Wellbeing requires sustainable change and daily practice.

Coaching for wellbeing

Coaching for wellbeing is a change-oriented, reflective and collaborative process focused on the subjective and personal exploration of factors that can contribute to enhancing an individual's sense of wellbeing. It tends to be psychological in nature and emphasises subjective experiences; among its objectives may be 'feeling good' and 'functioning well', considering both mental and physical components (Oades, 2015).

Although there can be an overlap between the coaching for wellbeing and health coaching, these are not interchangeable terms. Coaching for wellbeing tends to be multi-dimensional in its focus, going over and above managing illness or distress (Oades, 2015). It encompasses not only physical or mental health improvement but also interpersonal, social and psychological aspects of the human experience which impact individuals' sense of wellbeing. As a distinct coaching practice and research area, health coaching is concerned with health education, promotion and the improvement of health-related goals (Palmer et al., 2003). Health coaching tends to be applied in the context of self-management of long-term physical and mental health conditions and when the focus is the improvement of health outcomes. For example, helping people living with diabetes manage their glucose levels and sustain a lifestyle that keeps their diabetes under control. Motivational interviewing is one of the models extensively used by health coaches.

Another term that coaches in this field may come across is wellness. The Global Wellness Institute defines wellness as 'the active pursuit of activities, choices and lifestyles that lead to a state of holistic health'. There are some overlaps between wellbeing and wellness, such as consideration for emotional and mental aspects of the human experience but, ultimately, wellness emphasises physical health, prevention of ill health and healthy lifestyle choices, including self-care, fitness, nutrition and healthy living.

Despite similarities, health coaching, wellness coaching and wellbeing coaching can differ significantly in how the coaching itself is delivered to clients. This means that coaches looking to build their practice will also need to develop their knowledge and skills in these areas, according to their interests.

1.1 Motivational interviewing

Motivational interviewing (MI) is a client-centred approach that aims to elicit behaviour change by helping clients to explore and resolve ambivalence. A core principle of MI is that individuals are more likely to accept and act upon opinions that they voice themselves. Research has confirmed that the relationship between the practitioner's behaviour and the client's resistance is directly correlated – confrontation style correlating to the client's resistant behaviour and supportive style correlating to positive change-oriented behaviour (Bein et al., 1993). The MI practitioner facilitates by eliciting the client's motivation for change, while resolving ambivalence. The coach will help and empower the client to resolve ambivalence and create the mechanisms and steps to change.

Defining wellbeing

The focus of this book is on coaching for wellbeing, but what is wellbeing? Although the word wellbeing has become part of our daily lives, it is not that easy to define. Wellbeing is a complex and multi-faceted construct and the definitions presented here are a small sample of many existing ways of defining wellbeing. Reflecting on the complexity of this concept will help us consider our understanding and approach to coaching for wellbeing, and invite us to embrace other perspectives.

Wellbeing has been equated with optimal psychological functioning and experience (Ryan & Deci, 2001), with the presence of positive emotions and the absence of negative emotions (Diener, 2000), and with positive functioning and fulfilment (Ryff & Keyes, 1995).

The Oxford English Dictionary defines wellbeing as 'the state of being comfortable, healthy, or happy'. The questions that arise from this definition are:

- Can unhealthy people experience wellbeing?
- Can people have a sense of wellbeing when they are not happy? How about when they are not comfortable? (Assuming that we can agree on what 'comfortable' means.)
- Could there be examples of people who experience wellbeing but who do not meet these conditions?

What Works Wellbeing, a UK think tank, defines wellbeing using data from the (2010) Measuring National Wellbeing Programme at the UK Office for National Statistics survey: 'Wellbeing, put simply, is about "how we are doing" as individuals, communities and as a nation and how sustainable this is for the future' (whatworkswellbeing.org).

It defined wellbeing as having 10 broad dimensions, based on a survey of what matters most to people in the UK. These dimensions are: (1) the natural environment; (2) personal wellbeing; (3) our relationships; (4) health; (5) what we do; (6) where we live; (7) personal finance; (8) the economy; (9) education and skills; and (10) governance.

With wellbeing encompassing so many areas of people's lives, the focus of coaching for wellbeing can be equally complex and diverse. In this book, I explore wellbeing in its broadest sense. In my practice, I encourage clients to reflect on the many areas of their lives that impact their wellbeing and embrace that complexity, trusting that they will find the keys to creating and sustaining a flourishing life, and that they will also be able to find ways of living their lives to the full, even under challenging circumstances.

Wellbeing in organisations

In organisational settings, the profound changes in the workplace, brought about by the COVID-19 pandemic, led to a renewed interest in employees' wellbeing. The link between employee wellbeing, engagement and productivity (Boccoli et al., 2022) is not a new one.

As organisations contend with much more fluid work structures, including hybrid and remote working, and the impact these changes have on individuals, there is a significant need for organisations to improve their understanding of their employees' wellbeing needs and challenges, and to promote more positive work practices. Moreover, employees in some workplaces and industries are reporting increasingly higher levels of stress and burnout due to overwork and stress, with dire consequences not only for organisations but also for themselves, their families and communities.

1.2 A culture of overwork

Coaches working in organisations are probably familiar with challenges around overworking. Increasingly, more employees are experiencing stress and burnout resulting from unhealthy working practices. In 2021, a report published by the think tank Autonomy stated that UK workers had their workload increased by almost 25 per cent – a result of working from home during the pandemic. This seems to be a global issue. The first global analysis of the loss of life and health associated with working long hours, published in 2021 by the World Health Organisation and the International Labour Organisation (Pega et al., 2021), showed that 745,000 people died in 2016 from stroke and ischemic heart disease as a direct result of having worked at least 55 hours a week.

Worryingly, the WHO report shows this is a growing trend. It stated that the number of people working long hours is increasing, and currently stands at 9 per cent of the total population globally. Working long hours is now responsible for one-third of the occupational disease burden. The study concludes that working 55 or more hours per week is associated with an estimated 35 per cent higher risk of a stroke and a 17 per cent higher risk of dying from ischemic heart disease, compared to working 35–40 hours a week.

Unfortunately, this is not a new phenomenon. In Japan, the term *karoshi* (literally death by overwork) has been used for decades to describe the death of people working incredibly long hours (over 60 hours per week), leading to worker fatalities from heart failure, stroke or suicide. This culture of overwork is believed to have started after the Second World War as the country pulled together to rebuild itself. *Karoshi* continues to be a problem in Japan, with anti-*karoshi* campaigners putting the death toll at around 10,000 per year.

The paradox is that, while organisations seem to be more interested in supporting the wellbeing of employees, according to the Chartered Institute of Personnel and Development (CIPD, 2021), working practices are not always aligned or supportive of better wellbeing outcomes, a culture of overwork being a case in point.

Therefore, it is important to emphasise that coaching for wellbeing is no panacea. It can be a helpful tool and intervention to support individuals and teams in organisations but, alone, it cannot address systemic issues that are detrimental to the wellbeing of employees. Moreover, to maximise its effectiveness, coaching should be deployed as part of a well-thought-through wellbeing strategy that is integrated into the day-to-day workings of the business and embedded in the culture and leadership of the organisation.

The dark side of love

'Do what you love and you'll never have to do a day's work in your life.' Doing what we love, what gives purpose and what excites us can be incredibly energising and therefore supportive of our wellbeing. On the other hand, too much good work is still detrimental to our wellbeing and health. Unfortunately, research shows people whose work is driven by purpose can also be prone to workaholism and burnout (Duffy & Dik, 2013). This phenomenon can be seen across many industries but it is particularly associated with professionals working in a purpose-driven environment, such as in health and social care, education and in not-for-profit organisations (Duffy et al., 2018). A strong connection to their role and the outcomes of their work can make it difficult for them to create healthy boundaries between work and their personal lives and to switch off. Those engaged in meaningful work may find it easier to justify their overwork by rationalising the reasons for it.

Coaching as part of the wellbeing strategy

Organisations can develop their strategy around three key areas: physical wellbeing, psychological wellbeing and social wellbeing. The strategy needs to be informed by the needs of the company and its employees and, ideally, wellbeing initiatives will be designed to achieve specific goals, such as an increase in employee engagement; reduction in absenteeism; better staff retention; and higher levels of employee satisfaction. Having specific goals helps the organisation to evaluate the impact of the strategy. For each of the three areas above (and organisations may decide there are other areas they need to address), the strategy will include the tools that can be used to deliver the desired outcomes, and coaching for wellbeing can be one of them. As a flexible intervention, coaching can be used to support employees across these different areas. For example, one-to-one coaching can be helpful to support individuals' psychological needs, while group coaching can be deployed to improve inclusion and belonging, which is supportive of a better social work environment. Coaching for wellbeing can also help the organisation address specific employees' needs. For example, through programmes aimed at supporting parents or people living with a long-term condition (mindful of the remit of wellbeing coaching versus health coaching, which is addressed later in this chapter), or programmes targeted at managers and teams.

In an ideal world, all organisations, big and small, would invest time and resources in creating a robust wellbeing strategy, developed in partnership with employees, and which fits in with the organisation's ethos and vision. It will also have a framework for delivery and effective evaluation in place.

The reality is that coaches will find themselves working with organisations at distinct stages of development regarding their wellbeing thinking and strategy. This can have an impact on how coaches deliver the coaching and work with clients, as well as how coaches and organisations evaluate the coaching programme.

1.3 Examples of how coaching for wellbeing can be useful in organisations

- One-to-one coaching for individuals as part of an employee wellbeing/ assistance programme: People can sign up for the coaching programme any time they like; organisations can either offer unlimited coaching or a limited number of sessions over a period of time. Employees have flexibility in how they use these sessions, as long as they remain wellbeing-focused.

- One-to-one coaching programmes which are aligned to individuals' personal development plans and have specific overarching aims, such as support with a long-term condition or improving work-life balance. The objectives for these sessions are wellbeing-focused and they align with a development objective agreed between the employee and their manager.

- Group coaching around specific themes: Long-term conditions, parenting, work-life balance, managing stress/priorities, inclusion and belonging, developing positive habits, improving health, and so on. These can be offered as part of an employee wellbeing/assistance programme and open for people to sign up, according to their needs and interests, or as part of a worker's professional development plan.

- Group coaching for wellbeing: Generic offer that is open to individuals in the organisation who are interested in exploring their wellbeing in a more open way. These can be offered as above.

A systemic perspective

Some of the challenges linked to the wellbeing of staff and teams in organisations have their roots in systemic issues that are outside the individual's control. For example, workplaces that have practices which are not conducive to supporting staff's wellbeing, such as a culture of long hours, back-to-back calls with no breaks, or being overwhelmed due to unrealistic workloads and deadlines. Organisations need to ensure they walk the talk. If in one breath they are saying they are committed to employees' wellbeing but in the other, they do not challenge toxic management that lowers the workforce morale, then there won't be a real improvement in people's wellbeing. Strategies, policies and plans are crucial, but so is the relational space where work relationships and practices develop.

Although some of these pressures may be compounded by external circumstances, such as economic, political, social, and environmental factors, there could be room for improved practices.

Those responsible for the wellbeing of individuals and teams in organisations can in fact use coaching as a tool to help them develop and implement potential solutions and/or mitigating strategies across teams or organisations (Smith et al., 2021). The coaching can be used to bring together leaders and managers across functions and hierarchical boundaries to discuss unhelpful work practices and changes that can positively impact the wellbeing of staff members. Coaching can also be used to share best practice across the organisation, engage people in the conversation and explore their experience of barriers and enablers of wellbeing in their teams.

Recognising what is within the control of individuals and what is not is important. This helps people to explore the areas that can yield the greatest returns on their investment of time and effort, as well as identifying areas over which they may have influence, and those areas that are outside their control.

Organisations, especially those leading on wellbeing work, leaders and managers, will also benefit from understanding where their efforts are more likely to reap the benefits and the areas in which they can effect changes, while putting measures in place to mitigate the impact of things that may be outside their immediate control.

Examples of systemic solutions to support employees' wellbeing include a four-day week; the 'right to disconnect' from work emails outside working hours (which is bound by law in France, for example); flexible working hours and personal work arrangements to suit individuals; and by increasing the visibility of wellbeing by developing leaders and champions, whose role it is to support wellbeing across the organisation.

A four-day working week pilot lasting six months with 33 participating companies including the US, Australia, Ireland, the UK, New Zealand and Canada has returned some positive results. The pilot was led by a not-for-profit organization based in New Zealand and the data shows an increase in revenue for the participating companies and 67 per cent of employees reported being less burned-out.

Case study: Mila's story: an example of coaching for wellbeing in organisations

Mila came into coaching as part of an ad-hoc support programme put in place for employees of a large organisation. The coaching was not linked to a wellbeing strategy as this was being reviewed at the time. The organisation's broad aim for the coaching programme was simply 'to help employees improve their wellbeing'. Mila was a senior manager struggling to cope with an increasing workload, and managing an underperforming team, while caring for her ageing mother. She was feeling exhausted and drained, but she prided herself on being a high achiever. We contracted for six sessions on a monthly basis. The focus of the coaching at the beginning was more pragmatic as Mila explored strategies to cope with the pressures of daily life. Through the coaching process, which gave her time and space to think about her wellbeing in a more holistic and meaningful way, she decided to focus on rekindling her personal relationships, which had been neglected as work and caring demands increased. At the end of the coaching programme, one of the key changes for her was the quality of her relationship with her team, which had improved significantly. Devoting time and effort to her personal relationships led her to reconnect with a more playful part of herself, which she had 'forgotten even existed'. This made her reflect on and 'reset' the interactions with her team. She also managed to integrate a few positive self-care habits into her daily routine.

Wellbeing in communities

Outside organisational settings, coaching for wellbeing can be useful in various areas, including health, education, social care, and to support specific client groups, such as young people, the unemployed, and people from disadvantaged backgrounds (Nacif, 2021). Considering the positive impact good levels of wellbeing have on all aspects of people's lives, specific coaching for wellbeing programmes can be used to enhance existing community projects.

Living Well

Living Well, a London-based, not-for-profit health and wellbeing organisation specialising in supporting marginalised groups, such as ethnic minorities, LGBT+, women and those living with HIV, started to provide coaching as part of their services back in 2005. Today, coaching is an integral part of the organisation's health and wellbeing offer, which also includes counselling, peer support and wellbeing groups. The services are funded mainly through statutory bodies, such as the NHS and local authorities, and are intended to improve health and wellbeing, promote long-term life skills, encourage the development of a supportive social community, and empower participants with the ability to better self-manage their long-term conditions. Living Well's person-centred

Figure 1.1 Living Well's person-centred model

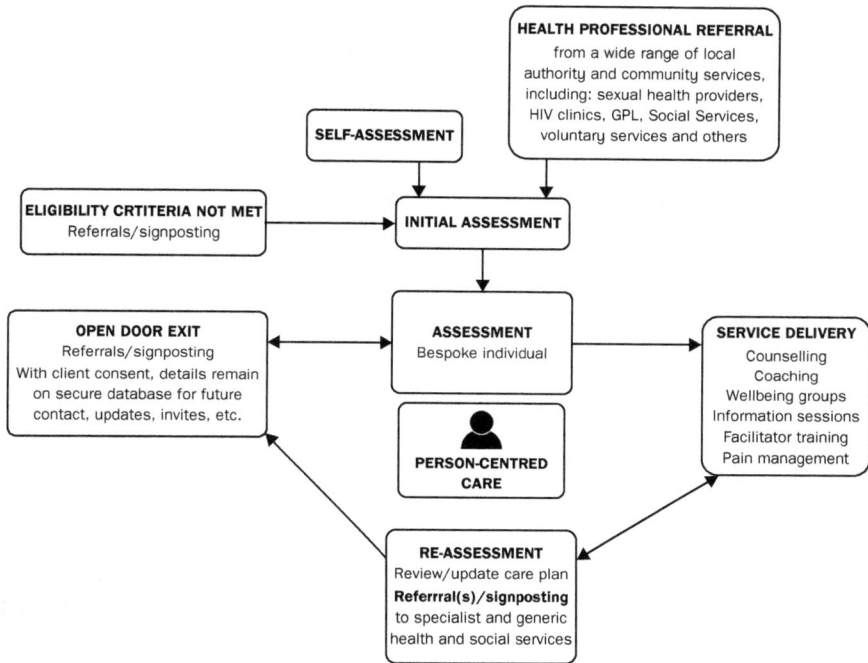

model (Figure 1.1) addresses physical, emotional (psychosocial) and psychological needs; conditions self-management; sex and relationships need; and social needs – as they relate to isolation and issues affected by HIV. The work of this organisation is a good example of how coaching for wellbeing can be used alongside other interventions to improve health outcomes.

Find Your Spark

Another organisation whose work includes coaching for wellbeing is *Find Your Spark*, a social enterprise initially set up in London in 2011. The organisation was set up by Michelle Shavdia to raise the wellbeing and resilience of at-risk secondary school children, using coaching. Michelle was an at-risk young person, being bereaved aged 14 when her dad died. The organisation has since evolved and is now based in Colchester, where it uses coaching and brief solution-focused therapy to support the wellbeing of primary school children who experience anxiety and/or who are neuro-divergent. Apart from supporting the children, the organisation also offers one-to-one and group coaching to parents. The mission of Find Your Spark is to raise awareness, acceptance and understanding so that neuro-divergent children and adults can feel accepted and understood, and have a sense of belonging, so that they can flourish.

Wellbeing paradigms

For millennia, human beings have been pondering what makes for a life that is lived well. Wellbeing, as a word or concept, is used pretty much in all spheres of our lives. But, despite being widely acknowledged and debated, it can be difficult to define (Dodge et al., 2012). In the Western world, Greek philosophers have set the ideas that inform the two major paradigms that have influenced empirical research on this topic, namely hedonism and eudaimonism. The hedonistic approach equates wellbeing with pleasure, pain avoidance and happiness (Diener et al., 1999), while eudaimonism sees wellbeing as the actualisation of human potential (Waterman, 1993). As summed up by Huta (2013): 'Hedonia is the pursuit of what feels good; eudaimonia is the pursuit of what one believes to be right' (p. 224).

The eudaimonic tradition comes from Aristotle's philosophy of happiness (4000 BC) as presented in his *Nicomachean Ethics*, where he articulates the ideas surrounding the 'good life', a life of virtue and excellence. Aristotle makes a distinction between pleasure (*hedonia*) and living well (*eudaimonia*), which implies pursuing excellence and actualising one's authentic and highest nature (*daimon*). In this context:

> Living well entails actively and explicitly striving for what is truly worthwhile and is of inherent or intrinsic human worth, and it contrasts with the pursuit of crass endeavours such as materialism or pleasure seeking that pull one away from virtues. Eudaimonia is characterized by reflectiveness and reason. Finally, eudaimonic pursuits are voluntary, and are expressions of the self rather than products of external control or ignorance.
>
> (Ryan et al., 2008, p. 145)

The difference between these two paradigms is the importance placed on pleasure and feelings of happiness (Figure 1.2), as opposed to thriving for achievement in life through discovering meaning and purpose, even when circumstances are not pleasant. From a eudaimonic perspective, there is more to wellbeing than happiness. These are important distinctions when we consider what wellbeing may mean for ourselves and our clients, and the paths we can choose to get there.

In terms of research and theories that can help inform our coaching practice, each paradigm has specific interests and therefore has produced distinct bodies of knowledge (Ryan & Deci, 2001). Research based on the hedonist view uses an assessment of subjective wellbeing (Diener, 1984), which consists of three components: (1) life satisfaction; (2) the presence of positive mood; and (3) the absence of negative mood. In short, how satisfied we feel with our lives and whether we experience more positive emotions than negative ones.

Figure 1.2 Wellbeing paradigms

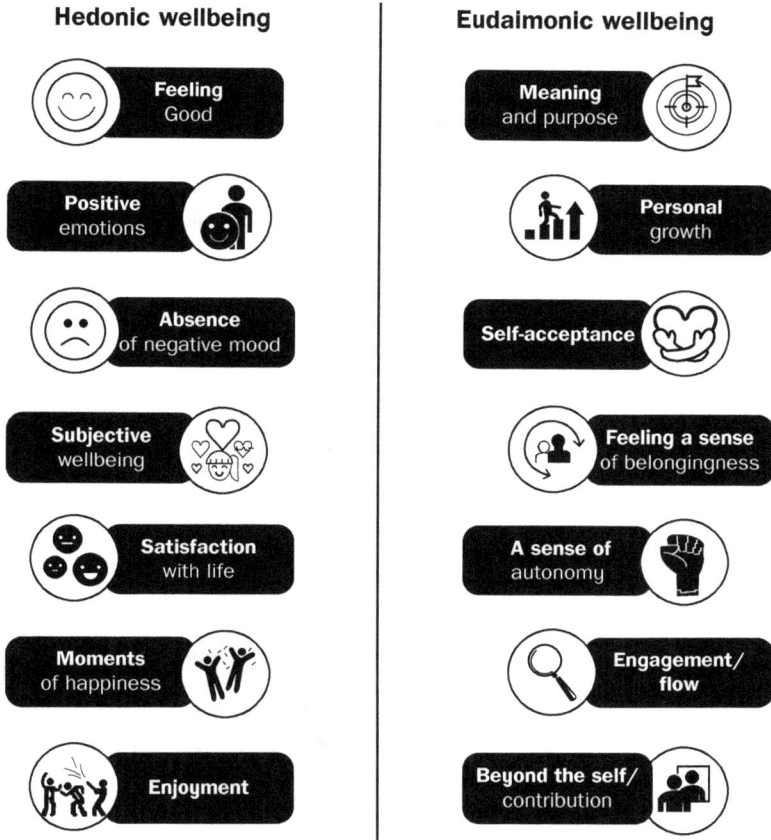

Hedonic wellbeing

Feeling Good

Positive emotions

Absence of negative mood

Subjective wellbeing

Satisfaction with life

Moments of happiness

Enjoyment

Eudaimonic wellbeing

Meaning and purpose

Personal growth

Self-acceptance

Feeling a sense of belongingness

A sense of autonomy

Engagement/ flow

Beyond the self/ contribution

1.4 The Satisfaction With Life Scale

This scale offers a snapshot of how satisfied someone is with their life overall, indicating their sense of subjective wellbeing. It was developed by researchers Diener, Emmons, Larsen, and Griffin and published in the *Journal of Personality Assessment* in 1985 (Diener et al., 1985).

It is a short questionnaire with only five statements. For each of these statements, those completing the questionnaire are asked to score themselves between 1 to 7, with 1 being 'strongly disagree' and 7 being 'strongly agree'. The scores are then combined to reveal the person's overall life satisfaction.

If you would like to try it out, here are the statements of the Satisfaction With Life Scale:

1 In most ways, my life is close to my ideal.
2 The conditions of my life are excellent.
3 I am satisfied with my life.
4 So far, I have gotten the important things I want in life.
5 If I could live my life over, I would change almost nothing.

What do the scores mean?

31–35 = Extremely satisfied
26–30 = Satisfied
21–25 = Slightly satisfied
20 = Neutral
15–19 = Slightly dissatisfied
10–14 = Dissatisfied
5–9 = Extremely dissatisfied

This scale is free for researchers and practitioners to use, as long as the authors of the scale are acknowledged.

Our overall sense of subjective wellbeing and our emotions are, of course, only one part of the story. From a eudaimonic point of view, wellbeing is about living a life of purpose and meaning. Conceptions of eudaimonia have varied more widely than those of hedonia. Huta and Waterman (2014) identified four core principles present across a range of eudaimonic concepts:

1 Authenticity (being true to one's true self and values)
2 Meaning (purpose in life, including beyond the self)
3 Excellence (accomplishment and high standard in performance and ethics)
4 Growth (fulfilling one's potential; personal learning and development)

Exploring wellbeing using both eudaimonia and hedonia brings to life the complexity of this construct. It is not a case of one or the other. Research shows that a combination of both approaches works, and individuals will experience a combination of eudaimonic and hedonic pursuits or activities. 'Under the right conditions, for example, priming positive emotions can lead to enhanced beliefs about the presence of meaning in life (King et al., 2006)' (Kashdan et al., 2008, p. 226).

What is important when working with our clients is that we help them explore different perspectives and potentially challenge the limitations of preconceived ideas: 'if a person does not have at least some hedonia and some eudaimonia, they may feel flat and unfulfilled, be more vulnerable to unhappiness, or develop psychopathology' (Huta, 2013, p. 225).

Our experience of wellbeing is dynamic and manifested in all aspects of our lives, including the following categories (Huta, 2013):

1 Orientation: What we want from life and why.
2 Behaviours: What we actually do on a day-to-day basis.
3 Experiences: Our typical feelings and emotions.
4 Functioning: How well we are doing in life.

To summarise: hedonic wellbeing focuses on enjoyment, pleasure and positive emotions, while eudaimonic wellbeing is more concerned with purpose and meaning. Reflecting on the principles behind these paradigms will help coaches better understand the foundations of wellbeing. In practice, both are useful and I will show you how we apply them in coaching in Chapter 3.

Eastern perspectives

The theories explored above have been mainly informed by Western philosophies, including an emphasis on positive emotions, optimal functioning, and individualistic concerns such as autonomy, self-esteem and self-efficacy, as opposed to a more collectivistic approach, which is more present in Eastern philosophies. The impact of this way of thinking is that coaching for wellbeing interventions are designed to support individuals, without considering the systemic factors that impact those individuals. Moreover, as practitioners we may not be thinking about a truly collective approach to wellbeing, for example, programmes that aim to tackle the wellbeing of whole communities and organisations. Even programmes that aim to generate a wider impact tend to use tools aimed at individual change. This poses some interesting and complex questions for coaching practitioners and their engagement beyond their professional practice.

We will not explore Eastern philosophies in depth in this book, but a brief overview will serve as a counterpoint to the theories discussed and will hopefully inspire further debate about our conceptualisation of wellbeing and how we interpret and support it.

Cultures based on individualistic philosophies tend to focus on individual agency, independence and the self, usually with a great and sometimes misconstrued leaning towards self-improvement, as an avenue to increased wellbeing and the good life. In Eastern cultures, there seems to be an importance placed on the collective (versus the individualistic ego), and mutual support, harmony, inter-dependency and a sense of wellbeing that are intrinsically linked to being fully immersed in the fabric of communities, their values and ethos. Moreover, in Eastern societies, transcendence and spirituality seem to be interwoven in concepts of happiness, wellbeing, contentment and fulfilment, in a way that is not present in the Western conceptualisations of wellbeing.

In his article, 'Eastern conceptualizations of happiness: Fundamental differences with Western views', Joshanloo (2014) explains, for example, how in

Hinduism joy comes from experiencing peace of mind 'by constantly acknowledging that in everything dwells the Supreme Being (Brahman)' (p. 478), which promotes an egoless state and virtues such as gratitude, non-violence, limitless compassion, and generosity.

In Buddhism, the path to fulfilment is one of balance and contentment, with a deep understanding of impermanence and practising detachment. This means that our Western understanding of positive emotions and hedonistic pleasure has no place in Buddhist philosophy, which also emphasises the collective nature of our human experience. 'Happiness understood in the Buddhist way is not necessarily incompatible with suffering, sadness, and tragedy (Ricard, 2011), considering that the Buddhist version of happiness is not premised on hedonic balance' (p. 479).

It is worth pointing out that the second wave of positive psychology, as well as humanistic and existential psychology, have promoted ideas of meaning and fulfilment which can be derived from adverse life experiences. If we pause our thoughts on wellbeing, as opposed to transitory feelings of happiness, then we can see some synergies, while acknowledging that these schools of thought come from different traditions.

In Taoism, the principle of non-action and of not actively favouring happiness may sound alien to Western-informed approaches. Contentment and peace of mind are highly valued in Taoism. Tao can be achieved by not favouring one side of the spectrum (happiness) over the other (suffering), and by acknowledging change is constant. Balance is also reflected in the idea that the positive is hidden in the negative and vice versa.

The differences between Western and Eastern ideas of happiness and wellbeing are complex and multi-faceted. It is illuminating to think about these different perspectives in our coaching practice and reflect upon our own personal and cultural biases and assumptions, which are also reflected in the theories and research we produce.

I am aware that this short section does not reflect the wealth and depth of Eastern approaches to wellbeing. However, I wanted to share some basic differences, which I hope have served as food for thought in your coaching practice as well as a topic for further reflection as you expand your understanding of wellbeing.

2 Wellbeing theories

In this chapter we will explore existing theories of wellbeing, which shed light on its various facets and how these building blocks can help us understand the dynamic nature of our personal wellbeing experience. Wellbeing theories tend to lean on the wellbeing paradigms we discussed in Chapter 1 as well as other psychological theories.

The wellbeing theories we will discuss are:

1 Psychological wellbeing theory
2 Positive psychology
3 Flow
4 Self-determination theory.

1 Psychological wellbeing theory

Psychological wellbeing theory (Ryff, 1989) has six dimensions: (1) purpose in life; (2) self-acceptance; (3) autonomy; (4) personal growth; (5) environmental mastery; and (6) positive relationships (Figure 2.1). It draws on various philosophical and psychological theoretical underpinnings, including developmental psychology – Bühler (1935), Massarik (1968), Erikson (1959) and Neugarten (1968); existential and humanist psychology – Allport (1961), Frankl (1992), Maslow (1968) and Rogers (1957); and clinical psychology – Jahoda (1958) and Jung (1933).

For Ryff (1989), wellbeing is closely related to more enduring life changes, such as having a sense of purpose and direction, achieving satisfying relationships and gaining a sense of self-realisation. The six constructs of psychological wellbeing are considered the foundation of the promotion of emotional and physical health. It draws on both eudaimonic and hedonic traditions, bringing together aspects of subjective wellbeing, such as happiness and life satisfaction as well as the six eudaimonic factors, as represented above.

The six dimensions of wellbeing (adapted from Ryff, 2014) are:

1 *Purpose in life*: How people perceive meaning, purpose and direction in their lives. 'This dimension of wellbeing draws heavily on existential perspectives, especially Frankl's search for meaning vis-à-vis adversity' (Frankl, 1985, p. 22). It is concerned with creating meaning even when life circumstances are extremely challenging. It is also about fully engaging with and living life with intention, and according to one's beliefs and purpose.

Figure 2.1 Six dimensions of psychological wellbeing

Source: Ryff (2014).

2 *Self-acceptance*: Positive self-regard; accepting oneself, including an awareness of one's limitations. 'This is defined as a central feature of mental health (Jahoda) as well as a characteristic of self-actualization (Maslow), optimal functioning (Rogers), and maturity (Allport)' (Frankl, 1985, p. 20).

3 *Autonomy*: People's ability to live according to their convictions; living life with self-determination and independence.

4 *Personal growth*: Using one's personal talents and potential. From aspects of wellbeing, this comes closest in meaning to Aristotle's eudaimonia and is concerned with self-realisation.

5 *Environmental mastery*: Ability to manage life situations.

6 *Positive relationships*: Meaningful connections with others; from aspects of well-being, concerned with self-realisation.

Ryff (2014) reviewed over 350 empirical studies on psychological wellbeing conducted in the preceding 25 years. She concluded that the evidence supports the benefits of psychological wellbeing to people's mental health. Weiss, Westerhof and Bohlmeijer (2016, p. 12) carried out a meta-analysis of the literature available on randomised trials of behavioural interventions aimed at improving psychological wellbeing and they concluded that it can be improved through behavioural interventions, including coaching, cognitive behavioural therapy (CBT), mindfulness and positive psychology programmes, among others.

Humanist psychology

Ryff's model was partly informed by the work of influential humanist psychologists of the twentieth century, including Jahoda (1958), Rogers (1957) and Maslow (1943). These well-known thinkers all used a person-centred eudaimonic perspective in their work when exploring the psychology of individuals and their ideas continue to influence psychological thinking to this day.

Until the humanists came along, the field of psychology was mainly focused on Freud's psychoanalytical views, which posited that human behaviours are partly motivated by unconscious desires, or the behaviourist school, which proposed that all behaviours are learned from our interaction with the environment around us, through conditioning and association. On the other hand, humanist psychology considered the whole person and focused on the positives of human nature.

Austrian psychologist Marie Jahoda was a trailblazer in her ideas about mental health, as she challenged the focus on mental disease, arguing for the importance of context and people's mental health and wellbeing. She devised a list of characteristics for ideal mental health (Jahoda, 1958):

- Efficient self-perception
- Realistic self-esteem and acceptance
- Voluntary control of behaviour
- True perception of the world
- Sustaining relationships and giving affection
- Self-direction and productivity.

Maslow's work on motivation was visionary. According to Maslow, human beings strive to self-actualise and to achieve their full potential, through internal and intrinsic needs. His hierarchy of needs theory (Maslow, 1943) states that there are specific categories we need to fulfil in order to achieve a higher order of needs, and eventually self-actualise. The needs are usually represented as a pyramid (Figure 2.2). The original five-stage model was expanded to include cognitive, aesthetic and transcendence needs.

Maslow originally stated that the lower needs must be satisfied before a person can move on to the next higher level but he eventually clarified (Maslow, 1987) that each tier of needs does not have to be totally met for a person to be able to strive for higher needs. He added that individual differences and circumstances mean that people may focus on specific needs more than others, creating their own hierarchical order. In addition, he explained that it is likely that we will tend to have a range of needs at the same time, in other words, most of our behaviours are multi-motivated.

This flexibility explains, for example, the poet whose creative genius is fully expressed as they experience loneliness and emotional turmoil; of those living in highly uncertain environments who can forge strong communities and a

Figure 2.2 Maslow's Hierarchy of Needs

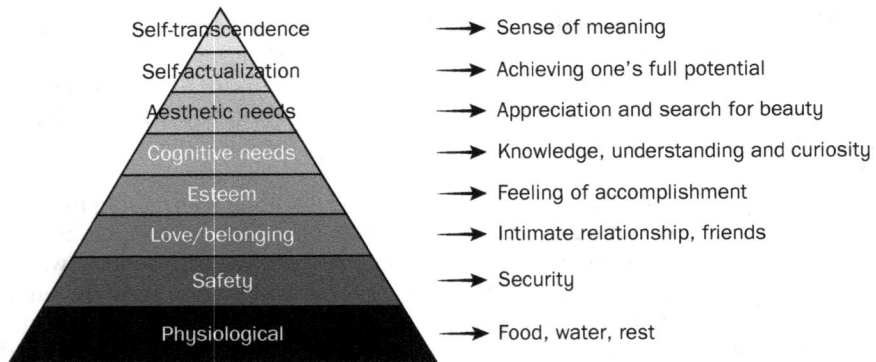

Self-transcendence ——▶ Sense of meaning

Self-actualization ——▶ Achieving one's full potential

Aesthetic needs ——▶ Appreciation and search for beauty

Cognitive needs ——▶ Knowledge, understanding and curiosity

Esteem ——▶ Feeling of accomplishment

Love/belonging ——▶ Intimate relationship, friends

Safety ——▶ Security

Physiological ——▶ Food, water, rest

Source: Maslow (1968).

sense of belonging, and so on. Another criticism of his theory was the lack of empirical evidence in support of it. However, findings in neuroscience support Maslow's ideas that the human brain has other motivational systems (Kenrick et al., 2010), unrelated to the reward system proposed by the behaviourists.

Jahoda's and Maslow's ideas are aligned to the eudaimonic tradition of human striving, which helps us explore paths for achieving wellbeing. Another important influence is Carl Rogers (1957), whose core conditions for therapeutic change are equally applicable to the field of coaching. These are: (1) congruence (being authentic); (2) unconditional positive regard (acceptance of the other person); and (3) empathic understanding (an ability to grasp the experience of another person).

2 Positive psychology

Humanistic psychology paved the way to positive psychology. Seligman and Csikszentmihalyi (2000) pioneered the principles of positive psychology, which were developed as an antidote to the focus of psychological research and practice on psychological dysfunction, as opposed to optimal functioning. Positive psychology draws on both hedonic and eudamoinic paradigms and is concerned with the flourishing and optimal functioning of people, groups and organisations (Gable & Haidt, 2005).

Well before the term positive psychology was coined by Seligman, some of its concepts were studied by Fordyce (1977, 1983), who developed the first-ever documented wellbeing intervention designed to increase happiness. Fordyce's (1977) experiment included 14 techniques, such as spending more time with others, enhancing close relationships, thinking positively, admiring and appreciating happiness, and refraining from worrying. He revisited the subject in 1983, with further research into a programme called *Fourteen Fundamentals* (of happiness), delivered across various cohorts with positive results.

The principles of positive psychology can be applied through positive psychology coaching (PPC) and positive psychology interventions (PPIs). Positive psychology coaching has been defined as

> coaching approaches that seek to improve short-term wellbeing (i.e. hedonic wellbeing) and sustainable wellbeing (i.e. eudaimonic wellbeing) using evidence-based approaches from positive psychology and the science of wellbeing – and enable the person to do this in an on-going manner after coaching has completed.
>
> (Passmore & Oades, 2014)

These authors state that positive psychology coaching follows four key positive psychological theories, namely: strengths theory, broaden-and-build theory (Fredrickson, 2004), self-determination theory (Ryan et al., 2008) and wellbeing theory (Seligman, 2012).

PERMA

Seligman's (2012) wellbeing theory, or PERMA, also draws on both hedonic and eudaimonic paradigms and proposes five dimensions that support flourishing and wellbeing. PERMA = (1) **P**ositive emotions; (2) **E**ngagement; (3) positive **R**elationships; (4) **M**eaning; and (5) **A**ccomplishment:

1 *Positive emotions*: This is linked to the hedonic paradigm and the idea of positive and pleasant feelings and experiences. Barbara Fredrickson's (2004) broaden-and-build theory suggests that positive emotions help us to broaden our horizons, experiences and resources.
2 *Engagement*: This is about becoming absorbed, present and immersed in what you are doing; this level of engagement in an activity has been described as a state of flow (Csikzentmihalyi, 1990).
3 *Positive relationships*: These represent all the interactions we have with others in our personal and professional lives where we feel valued, loved and cared for. Humans are inherently social and the quality of our connections to others has an impact on our lives and wellbeing.
4 *Meaning*: This dimension is more aligned with the eudaimonic tradition and it is about finding meaning and purpose in life; living life according to our values and feeling connected to something bigger than ourselves.
5 *Accomplishment*: This is about a sense of achievement that can be derived from making progress towards something we want and reaching our goals, personal or professional. Accomplishments can be big or small, and in any sphere of life.

Since Seligman developed PERMA, other researchers have explored additional dimensions that could support positive functioning and flourishing. Donaldson and Donaldson expanded the model to create a holistic framework for work-related wellbeing and work performance, creating the PERMA+4 model

(Donaldson & Donaldson, 2021). The four dimensions added to the model were: (1) physical health; (2) mindset; (3) work, environment; and (4) economic security.

1 *Physical health*: A combination of high levels of biological, functional, and psychological health assets.
2 *Mindset*: Adopting a growth mindset characterised by an optimistic, future-oriented view of life, where challenges or setbacks are seen as opportunities to grow.
3 *Work environment*: Quality of physical work environment and a positive psychological climate.
4 *Economic security*: Perceptions of financial security and stability.

We will look at the application of PERMA in more detail in Chapter 3, where we explore how wellbeing theories can be applied in practice.

Positive psychology interventions

Positive psychology principles can be applied through positive psychology interventions (PPIs), defined as treatment methods or intentional activities that aim to cultivate positive feelings, behaviours, or cognitions (Sin & Lyubomirsky, 2009). Positive psychology interventions are based on various constructs, such as gratitude, hope, goal attainment, compassion, humour, and kindness; a number of studies have looked into their effectiveness (Seligman et al., 2005).

PPIs have been widely researched with some results showing they can have a positive impact on people's wellbeing (Seligman et al., 2005). Giannopoulos and Vella-Brodrick (2011) compared the impact of positive psychology interventions (pleasure, engagement, meaning or a combination) on 218 people and concluded that wellbeing increased in all intervention conditions.

In an online positive psychology intervention study of 1624 adults, Gander et al. (2016) concluded that 'interventions based on pleasure, engagement, meaning, positive relationships, and accomplishment are effective strategies for increasing wellbeing and ameliorating depressive symptoms and that positive psychology interventions are most effective for those people in the middle range of the wellbeing continuum' (p. 686).

Examples of PPIs are gratitude interventions, which may involve self-reflective practice, such as a gratitude journal, or action-oriented interventions, such as writing a thank-you letter (Snyder & Lopez, 2009). Other PPIs may involve kindness practices, mindfulness, identifying and using strengths, finding meaning in daily activities, and practising savouring moments, among others (Snyder & Lopez, 2009). PPIs have been widely researched and many meta-analyses confirmed that they can be used effectively to enhance people's wellbeing (Bolier et al., 2013; Carr et al., 2021; Sin & Lyubomirsky, 2009).

Broaden-and-build theory of positive emotions

This theory (Fredrickson, 2004) posits that positive emotions broaden and expand our attention, cognition, and receptivity to experiences, helping us build social, emotional and physical resources. Unlike negative emotions, which narrow our perspectives and ideas about potential actions to resolve an issue or to create something new, positive emotions, such as joy, interest, contentment, pride and love, do exactly the opposite. They help us to expand our thought–action repertoires, which leads us to more ideas and a wider range of possibilities and actions available to us at any given time. As we explore a wider range of possibilities, we build our personal resources (physical, intellectual, social and psychological), such as skills, knowledge and resilience. These resources allow us to achieve more and expand our thinking, which in turn creates emotions that are more positive.

According to Fredrickson, positive emotions also enable individual growth and social connection, as well as improving people's lives. Her research showed that positive emotions not only broaden people's thought–action repertoires, these emotions also undo lingering negative emotions and build psychological resilience, triggering upwards spirals towards enhanced emotional wellbeing (Fredrickson & Joiner, 2002).

Second-wave positive psychology

The second wave in positive psychology (or PP2.0) recognises that positive and negative psychological states and experiences cannot be polarised and need to be seen as part of the whole person. As a result, it leans towards a more existential lens that uses meaning and purpose as pathways to wellbeing. Under PP2.0 (Wong, 2011), meaning can be aligned to the logotherapy theory, developed by Viktor Frankl, which also informed Ryff's (1989) model, as seen above.

Logotherapy theory is founded on the belief that striving to find meaning is one of the key drivers in human nature. According to Frankl (1985), a clear sense of meaning and purpose can add something positive and significant to one's life, regardless of circumstances and health conditions. Meaning is a *sine qua non* for the eudaimonic concept of wellbeing, which calls upon people to live by their daimon, or true self (Waterman, 1993). However, there are diverse ways of exploring meaning, meaning-seeking and meaning-making. Whereas meaning-making models focus on making sense of the world in negative situations, the meaning-seeking model focuses more on how to live with courage, freedom and responsibility (Wong, 2014). Meaning-seeking is primarily about how to live a life of significance and purpose. Two logotherapy concepts are particularly useful to understand in relation to this principle: freedom to will and will to meaning. 'Freedom to will' is Frankl's hypothesis that 'one always has the freedom of choice, at least in attitude if not in action' (Wong, 2014, p. 161) and the 'will to meaning means that each individual is motivated to discover his or her unique life calling' (Wong, 2014, p. 152). These distinctions are very helpful, especially when coaches work with people who are experiencing challenging life circumstances.

In addition, the second wave also discusses how we can flourish through suffering, which may be incredibly important when working with clients whose lives are exceptionally hard, such as those in palliative care, those who have experienced trauma and/or major disasters. Wong (Wong et al., 2021) explains that there are four ways in which we flourish through suffering:

1 Suffering makes us search for meaning in life.
2 It motivates us to embrace sacrifice to make our lives more meaningful and worthwhile.
3 It teaches us how to overcome painful experiences to live a better life.
4 It contributes to personal growth.

He explains that suffering provides new ground for hope and happiness, and that sustainable wellbeing can be achieved through learning how to make the best use of the dynamic between positive and negative life experiences.

3 Flow

Mihaly Csikszentmihalyi introduced flow theory in the 1970s. He defined flow, or peak experience, as

> a state in which people are so involved in an activity that nothing else seems to matter; the experience is so enjoyable that people will continue to do it even at great cost, for the sheer sake of doing it.
>
> (Csikszentmihalyi, 1990, p. 4)

Flow is usually referred to as 'being in the zone' and being totally immersed in something. We are so engaged in whatever activity we are doing that our sense of time becomes distorted, and time passes without us realising it. Another characteristic of flow is that 'self-consciousness' disappears, which means there is no interference from our mind chatter or worrying about failure; it is a state which puts our thinking mind on hold. To achieve flow, we need to have clear goals and create the right balance between challenge and skill. Too much challenge and we enter the anxiety zone, too little and we end up in apathy (Figure 2.3).

Flow is dynamic. The level of complexity of the activity should increase over time as we develop the skills to meet current challenges, keeping us engaged and inspired to continue improving. As we experience activity and we develop the necessary skills to meet the current challenges, the level of complexity should increase over time, keeping us engaged.

Thus, flow is a dynamic rather than a static state, since a properly constructed flow activity leads to increased skill, challenge, and complexity over

Figure 2.3 Flow model

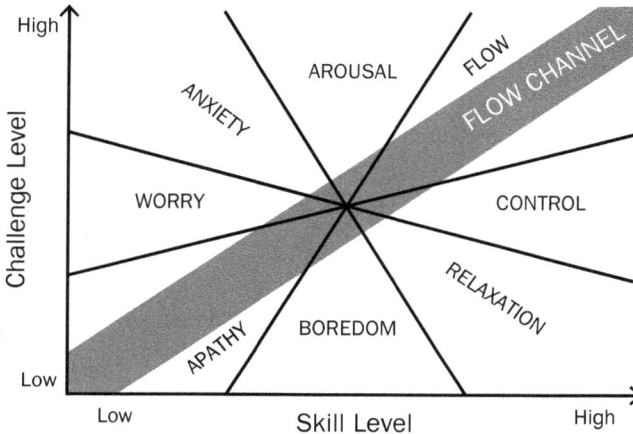

Source: Adapted from Csikszentmihalyi (1990).

time. Since one's skill does not remain static, repeating the same activity would fall into boredom; the flow reward inspires one to face harder challenges.

Examples of activities that may induce a flow state are sports, gaming, creative pursuits such as music, art and dance, and outdoor activities. Remember that, to get into flow, the following conditions need to be met:

- There are clear goals every step of the way.
- There is immediate feedback on one's actions.
- There is a balance between challenges and skills.
- Action and awareness are merged.
- Distractions are excluded from consciousness.
- There is no worry of failure.
- Self-consciousness disappears.
- The sense of time becomes distorted.
- The activity becomes an end in itself.

According to Csikszentmihalyi, some people have an autotelic self, which enables them to become deeply involved in whatever they are doing. He mentions five steps to cultivate an autotelic self:

1 Setting goals that have clear and immediate feedback.
2 Becoming immersed in the particular activity.
3 Paying attention to what is happening in the moment.
4 Learning to enjoy immediate experience.
5 Proportioning one's skills to the challenge at hand.

4 Self-determination theory

Self-determination theory (STD) (Ryan & Deci, 2000) is a framework for the study of human motivation and personality. It suggests that people can become self-determined when their psychological needs for competence, relatedness, and autonomy are met. The satisfaction of these basic and universal needs also fosters personal growth and wellbeing:

- *Autonomy*: Having choice and volition over one's behaviours, goals and the ability to make their own decisions.
- *Competence*: A sense of efficacy and having the skills needed to be successful and to achieve the goals they set out for themselves.
- *Relatedness*: Feeling connected to other people with a sense of belonging and attachment to others.

STD assumes that people are naturally interested in growth and this need for growth drives our behaviour. And while it recognises that people may be motivated by external rewards (extrinsic motivation), such as money and status, it focuses on internal sources of motivation, such as personal satisfaction and independence (intrinsic motivation).

Part 2

Coaching for wellbeing: Bringing theory to life

In Part I, we considered the two paradigms that informed the conceptualisation of wellbeing and looked at theories that were developed to shed light on related experiences. Part II is about putting theory into practice and looking at how existing research in coaching for wellbeing can help us improve our practice.

3 Coaching for wellbeing in practice

In this chapter we are putting the wellbeing theories into practice.

Wellbeing vision

First, let's revisit what coaching for wellbeing is: a change-oriented, reflective and collaborative process focused on the subjective and personal exploration of factors that can contribute to enhancing an individual's sense of wellbeing. It tends to be psychological in nature and emphasises subjective experiences; among its objectives may be 'feeling good' and 'functioning well', considering both mental and physical components (Oades, 2015). This definition is sufficiently broad to accommodate the needs of clients from all walks of life, both individuals and organisations.

If we agree that the main objective of coaching for wellbeing is to support individuals to flourish and that experiences of wellbeing are highly subjective and complex, the starting point is to understand: (1) the client's perception of wellbeing (what wellbeing means to them), and (2) their wellbeing vision (if everything was possible, what would be their experience of wellbeing?). There is no rush at all in this initial stage to discuss specific goals – more about goals later in this chapter. The aim here is to fully understand the client's personal experience, knowledge and feelings about their wellbeing and invite them to imagine the best possible scenario, in the form of a compelling vision that excites them.

This first stage of the coaching process is also invaluable to developing the so-important relationship with your client. This is where your coaching skills of listening deeply, building trust, being present, curious and caring, designing the coaching alliance and holding a reflective space for your client will be most useful. In addition, this provides an opportunity to understand the areas of the client's life that positively and negatively affect their wellbeing, as well as the things that matter most to them.

You can use your preferred coaching tools to support the client with their wellbeing vision. Here are a few of the tools I have used in the past:

- *Vision board*: Ask your client to collect images, quotes, photographs, and objects which represent their wellbeing and create a board in an accessible place. This can be done on a physical board or online.

- *Visualisation*: Talk your client through a visualisation focused on taking them to their best life/sense of wellbeing.
- *Ideal day exercise*: With a particular focus on wellbeing, encourage your client to describe their ideal day.
- *Wellbeing story*: Invite the client to write a story about themselves, from the perspective of experiencing flourishing and wellbeing.

Why is having a vision so important? According to Intentional Change Theory, goal-setting works best when aligned to what matters most to the individual: 'When intentional change begins by connecting to the Ideal Self [who I want to be], the change process becomes grounded in intrinsic motivation, personal passion, resonant meaning, and belief in possibility' (Boyatzis & Howard, 2013, p. 215).

According to this theory, sustained change is moved by vision, which drives change by focusing the person's attention and energizing the person both psychologically and physiologically (p. 218). It turns out that an inspiring vision, based on what is important to us, and a good dollop of self-efficacy can really make a difference. Therefore, it is important to work with our clients on uncovering what is truly important to them and to help them shape their goals accordingly. Sometimes people are side-tracked by background noise and external pressure and lose touch with what they genuinely want and value.

The wheel of wellbeing

The wheel of wellbeing is similar to the wheel of life. It is a tool coaches use to get a snapshot of the client's satisfaction in various aspects of their lives (career, money, health, friends & family, significant other/romance, personal growth, fun & leisure, and physical environment). This tool includes the main factors that contribute to wellbeing and is very flexible.

You can populate the wheel using a particular model, such as PERMA (Seligman, 2018) or psychological wellbeing (Ryff, 1989). The variations are many, with some wellbeing wheels including aspects such as community, environment, body/physical health, mind, and financial wellbeing, to name just a few. Another option (which I tend to favour) is to work with the client on the areas they perceive as impactful to their wellbeing and pop these on an empty wheel. (There is a blank version of the wheel of wellbeing in the Appendix toolkit at the end of this book.) The wheel becomes a personalised tool they can use throughout the coaching. If the client has an extensive list of 'wellbeing areas', you can help them group them into clusters. Six to eight sections are probably enough.

Here are examples of typical areas for a wellbeing wheel:

- *Existential*: Living according to one's values; finding meaning and purpose in life; being in touch with things, people, activities that bring joy; being part of something bigger than oneself.

- *Mind*: Levels of stress and anxiety; growth mindset, and helpful thinking patterns/style, as well as learning.
- *Emotions*: Day-to-day emotional experience and ability to express and self-regulate emotions.
- *Relationships*: Friends and family; romantic relationships; being part of a supportive network of people; feeling connected to others.
- *Community*: This can be either related to a person's neighbourhood and local environment, or communities they belong to, either linked to their professional or personal interests.
- *Financial*: Practical issues related to their finances; ability to support oneself and/or cope with financial challenges.
- *Environment*: The physical environment in which someone lives, whether it is healthy, comfortable, and safe; it could be both home and neighbourhood.
- *Physical health*: Levels of exercise and physical activity that are suitable for each individual; energy levels; healthy eating and quality sleep.

Case study: John's life balance

John sought out coaching as he felt his energy levels dipping and he lacked motivation in his work and personal life. Since the pandemic, he has been working mainly from home and has found it difficult to keep a healthy boundary between his work and personal life. He's been working long hours as he is constantly attempting to reduce his ever-growing to-do list. This means missing out on socialising with friends and not spending quality time with his wife. He feels exhausted after a long day at work and has lost his zest for life.

We did not complete John's wheel of wellbeing until session three of his six-session coaching programme. We spent the first two sessions working on his wellbeing vision and discussing quick-win strategies to get him into a more productive place to contemplate his options for the future. He did a values exercise and realised that he had been neglecting three of his top five values: contribution, adventure and love. When I invited him to create his wellbeing wheel, he decided to include the segments detailed in Figure 3.1. His top priority was to restore some sense of adventure in his life, which had all but disappeared since the pandemic, contributing to him feeling lethargic and 'stuck'. A keen mountaineer, he decided to prioritise getting outdoors with his partner on weekends and organise their next 'big trip'. Although he found it difficult at the beginning to feel motivated, he persevered and, with the help of his partner, established a routine that worked for both of them. Reconnecting with his passion for the outdoors and his sense of 'adventure' had a positive ripple effect on his life.

Figure 3.1 John's personal wellbeing wheel

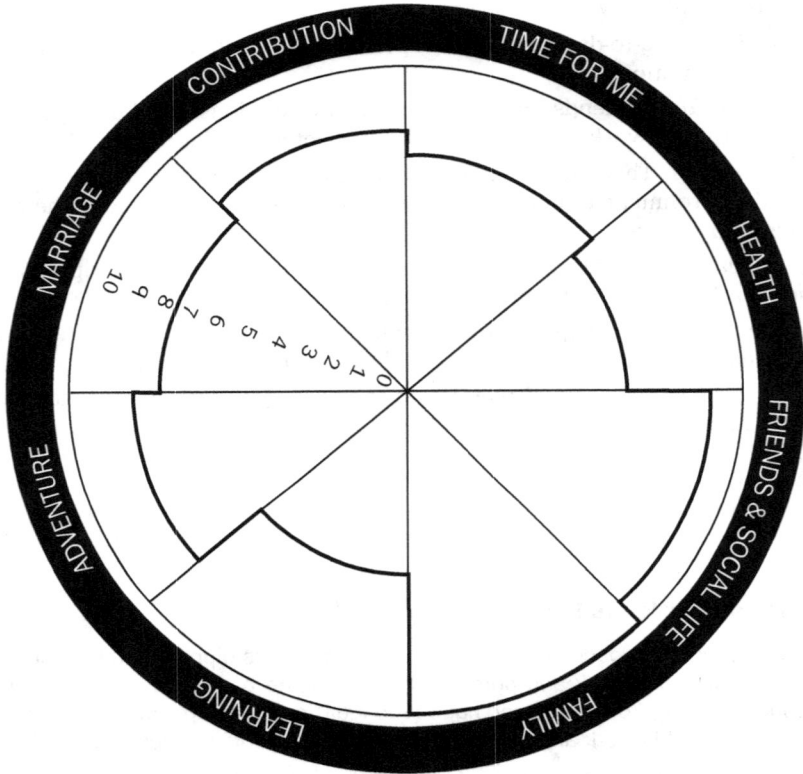

Balanced life

The idea of a perfectly balanced life can be appealing, but it is important to remember that a wheel of wellbeing does not have to be balanced at all. We are not looking for perfection. In fact, perfection can be the enemy of wellbeing. Striving to have a perfect life can put a lot of strain on individuals (Byrne, 2005). Life is always in flux and wellbeing is a constant journey, not a destination. Coaches need to refrain from 'assessing' their clients' lives based on the scores in the wheel of wellbeing. People may decide to focus on specific areas of their wellbeing and not others. Wellbeing choices are likely to be fluid and ever-changing. As clients raise their awareness of their wellbeing levels, and of the aspects of their lives that contribute to or hinder their wellbeing (the areas they feel are more pressing than others are), they will likely be considering not only wellbeing goals but also the impact of the choices they make on a daily basis.

Whereas in other areas of their lives, clients may have specific goals they want to achieve within a time frame (e.g., get a promotion within three years of joining a company), wellbeing is a lifetime pursuit. Our levels of wellbeing will likely impact our ability to pursue the goals we may have in other areas.

Figure 3.2 Jigsaws of wellbeing: what is yours like?

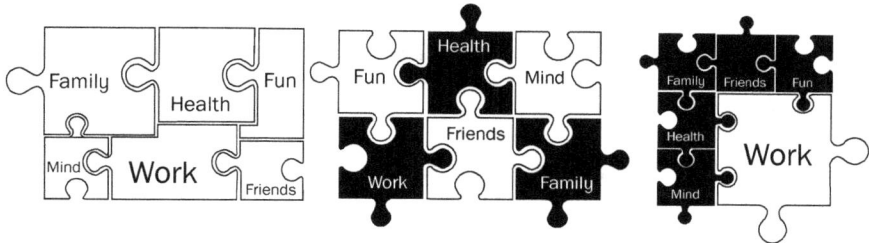

Wellbeing is not something we do on Monday and we are done for the week. It is complex and touches all aspects of our lives. Wellbeing goals may involve change that needs to happen over time to become sustainable; others require us to rethink long-standing habits and/or challenge how we think and interact in the world. Wellbeing is like an experiential jigsaw with ever-moving pieces that can be slotted in, moved and adapted to create different images (Figure 3.2).

Not only will some of these changes require effort and time, but trying to change too many things at once may have a detrimental impact on people's wellbeing, especially if they feel 'overwhelmed' by all the wellbeing stuff they 'need to do'. Here is an example of how a client of mine was feeling overwhelmed by her 'wellbeing list of things to do' and how she solved that problem.

Case study: Lucy's story

Lucy's daily wellbeing to-do lists read something like this: Yoga (1 hour), cooking at least one meal from scratch a day (1 hour, including sourcing ingredients – this could take even longer depending on the menu); meditation (30 minutes); read for pleasure (30 minutes); talk to a friend (30 minutes); paint (30 minutes); write a reflective journal (15 minutes). More generically, she also had on her list to spend quality time with her children and partner. All good for wellbeing, right? Of course, but instead of feeling energised and content, Lucy found herself totally exhausted trying to keep up with her schedule. She also felt frustrated as some of these activities kept being postponed to the next day, only to be neglected once more as life got in the way. This is not to say that Lucy won't be able to build these things into her life, but she had to consider her choices. She settled for a much wider time span to do the things she wanted to do so, for example, swapping 'daily' for 'weekly' or every few days, 'weekly' for 'fortnightly' and dropping some items off the list altogether. She decided she wanted more spontaneity in her life which meant fewer scheduled activities and more 'buffer time' to enjoy being in the moment, instead of rushing from one thing to another.

GREAT DREAM

Another wellbeing model, used by Action for Happiness, an organisation set up in 2010 whose mission is 'to promote a happier world through a culture that prioritises happiness and kindness', identified the 10 Keys to Happier Living (King et al., 2016), which together spell GREAT DREAM:

Giving: do things for others
Relating: connect with people
Exercising: take care of your body
Awareness: live life mindfully
Trying out: keep learning new things

Direction: have goals to look forward to
Resilience: find ways to bounce back
Emotions: look for what's good
Acceptance: be comfortable with who you are
Meaning: be part of something bigger

Each of these keys is portrayed in an action-oriented way, which nudges us to think about what we can do to activate them. They can serve as the basis of coaching conversations, but also as reminders for clients in their day-to-day life of the things that can contribute to their wellbeing.

Coaching with PERMA

By choosing to use the PERMA theory (see Chapter 2), you will focus the client's attention on the five dimensions of the model. The client can add other dimensions to it, particularly if there are areas of their wellbeing not represented in the model. For example, one of the gaps in this model is the absence of health as a dimension of wellbeing, which has led to some practitioners modifying the model by adding +H to it, creating PERMA + H. If you are working with organisations, there is the option of using PERMA+4, as described in Chapter 2.

You can present the model to the client as a framework for the coaching programme, giving them the flexibility to work as much or as little as they like in each dimension. It is worth considering each section carefully with the client to establish areas that:

- Can have the biggest impact on their wellbeing and/or take them closer to their wellbeing vision
- Can provide quick wins in terms of improving the quality of their everyday living
- Are least/most challenging
- Are most inspiring.

From the initial exploration, the client can set goals and/or outcomes for each area. They may have specific targets they want to achieve, for example, to join an art class to bring more enjoyment and flow to their lives. They may also be looking to create and embed healthier, more positive habits into their daily lives, such as exercising more regularly or being more present. The coaching acts as an exploratory effort to help them understand the impact of each of these areas in their lives and what is important to them. Let's take a look at each dimension separately. Remember, PERMA means:

P = positive emotions
E = engagement
R = positive relationships
M = meaning
A = accomplishment

Positive emotions

Some of us are more in touch with our emotions than others and, because of negativity bias (Rozin & Royzman, 2001), our perception of negative emotions may be stronger or more noticeable to us than our experience of positive emotions. Negativity bias also explains why we may pay more attention to negative events and dwell on them for longer. The focus is on increasing the client's experience of positive emotions, such as joy, love, inspiration, calmness, gratitude, and hope, among others. Some clients don't experience enough positive emotions in their lives; for others, these emotions are present but, because of the pull of the negativity bias, they barely notice them. As you coach them in this area, you will encourage the identification of more opportunities to experience positive emotions. Equally, you may be working with your client on their emotional responses to life circumstances, looking at whether there may be room for them to interpret events from a different, and perhaps more helpful, perspective. In his book, *Flow*, Csikszentmihalyi talks about people who are able to control their inner experience to determine the quality of their lives (1990, p. 2). This is summed up by the common phrase, 'It is not what happens to us, but how we interpret what happens to us or how we react to what happens to us that will impact our lives.' Working with clients on their emotional landscape and raising awareness of the role of emotions on their quality of life can help them increase their wellbeing. It is also interesting to note the link between positive mood and meaning. Research has shown that people who experience happiness and enjoyment are more likely to perceive their lives as meaningful (King et al., 2006). There are positive psychology interventions that can support this work and there are quick wins, accessible to virtually everyone. I share a few of these interventions later in this chapter.

Although this dimension of PERMA is an invitation to foster positive emotions, coaches need to be mindful that we are not advocating 'positive emotions at all costs', neither are we asking clients to reframe every negative experience they have. Emotions are fundamental to our wellbeing. They serve as a road map to our human experiences and give us information about ourselves and others, and the events around us. There are moments in life when it is appropriate to feel anger, sadness, grief, frustration and other so-called negative emotions. I think a better way to think about these emotions is to recognise that they are uncomfortable, as opposed to labelling them negative. Our job as wellbeing coaches is to hold the space for our clients and sometimes that space will be used to share and explore these uncomfortable emotions. The eudaimonic paradigm of wellbeing and the second-wave positive psychology can be particularly helpful in these circumstances. Wellbeing derived from personal growth, meaning, and purpose can surely come from life's most profound and transformative experiences, some of which are neither comfortable nor pleasant.

3.1   Moments of joy

What are your daily moments of joy? This is a great question to ask to get people to think about their everyday experiences and notice these moments. The objective here is not to create special moments, although these are wonderful too, of course, but to notice and savour fleeting moments of joy. The opportunities for positive experiences are endless, but here are a few examples that clients have shared with me over the years:

- The first cup of coffee in the morning, preferably in silence while the household is still and quiet.
- The smell of my child's hair.
- Feeling the warmth of the sun on my face.
- The sound and smell of the ocean on my morning walk with my dog.
- Sitting in my garden for five minutes before getting back to 'busy work'.
- Getting into a warm bath.
- A cup of tea, any time of the day.
- Watching the birds outside my window.
- Finishing a spinning class.
- Sitting by the fire in the winter.
- Hearing the sounds of the rain or wind outside.
- Being in prayer.
- Listening to my favourite song.
- Taking a moment for myself.
- The weight of my head against the cold pillow before I fall asleep.

You should encourage your clients to notice similar moments of joy in their daily routine. The less complicated and time-consuming they are, the better.

Apart from moments of joy, clients can also think about activities that make them feel good, for example, spending time with loved ones; engaging in fun and/or creative activities; listening to uplifting music, and being in nature.

Engagement

This dimension of the model is similar to experiencing flow, as described in Chapter 2. Being engaged means being totally immersed in our experience. One way of fostering flow is by using our strengths (Falecki et al., 2018).

You can share the concept of flow with clients and ask them to think about an instance when they lost track of time while totally immersed in a specific activity. Some clients will be able to immediately identify activities that give them that sense of flow, while others may need time to discover and try different things. A good starting point may be long-lost hobbies and passions that got side-lined to make space for other interests and tasks, perhaps interests they had as children or at a younger age.

We can think about the *body in flow* and the *mind in flow* or both. That, combined with the need for focus, a clear goal, skill-challenge dynamic and on-time feedback, leads us to activities that would be naturally conducive to flow, such as sports, games, martial arts, dance, arts, creative hobbies, crafts, music, solving puzzles, baking, to name just a few.

Strengths and flow

Another way to create states of flow is through our strengths, which can be broadly defined as natural talents and skills. One way of exploring strengths is identifying and using our character strengths. The concept of character strengths was developed by Peterson and Seligman (2004), who carried out research on strengths across cultures, which culminated in the VIA (Values in Action) classification. The VIA Character Strengths framework has 24 strengths, clustered around six virtues (Table 3.1).

You can complete the VIA Survey of Character Strengths for free at: https://www.viacharacter.org/

We all have all these 24-character strengths to a greater or lesser extent. Research shows that identifying and using our strengths has a positive impact

Table 3.1 The VIA Character Strengths framework

Wisdom	Courage	Humanity	Justice	Temperance	Transcendence
Creativity	Bravery	Kindness	Fairness	Forgiveness	Appreciation of beauty
Curiosity	Perseverance	Love	Leadership	Humility	Gratitude
Judgement	Honesty	Social intelligence	Teamwork	Prudence	Hope
Love of learning	Zest			Self-regulation	Humour
Perspective					Spirituality

on our wellbeing and life satisfaction. Using our strengths not only increases our level of engagement, but also has a positive impact on our emotions, giving us a sense of accomplishment and satisfaction. We can use our strengths to boost our energy levels and feel more confident and resilient; to sum up, strengths help us feel good about ourselves.

Practical strategies for engagement

Ask clients to complete the VIA survey and use coaching to explore their top strengths. Look at how they use them and encourage clients to engage with their strengths on a regular basis.

Explore the clients' passions and activities within which they could immerse themselves. Support clients to come up with strategies for 'being in the moment' and more present in their daily activities.

These are only a few suggestions. Work with your client to explore what is right for them.

Relationships

Social relationships provide physical and psychological benefits in many ways, including social support during times of stress, a sense of identity, and an overall boost to self-esteem (Baumeister & Leary, 1995).

Humans are social beings and relationships are fundamental to our wellbeing. Being in the company of others, interacting, sharing and celebrating together can change our outlook and boost our mood. Social connections give us a sense of being supported, cared for, and valued by other people. They also give us the opportunity to do the same for others, which has a positive impact on our wellbeing.

Relationships in the PERMA model can be any type of relationship: romantic ones, friendships, social networks built around a shared interest, and social peer groups that focus on shared experiences, such as parenting or living with a long-term health condition, for example.

When using the PERMA model, clients can reflect on existing relationships, and the quality of those relationships, as well as opportunities to connect with more people in a meaningful way.

Meaning

Meaning is about purpose, living life according to our values and feeling connected to something bigger than ourselves. Research has demonstrated that experiencing meaning in our lives increases our sense of wellbeing. Increased meaning has been associated with higher life satisfaction (Steger, 2018), self-esteem (Ryff, 1989), lower rates of anxiety and depression (Steger et al., 2006) and better physical health (Steger et al., 2009). All good reasons to help our clients explore this area. Meaning can have three clearly defined facets: coherence, purpose and significance (Martela & Steger, 2016):

Purpose refers to having goals and direction in life. Significance entails the degree to which a person believes his or her life has value, worth, and importance. Coherence, characterized by some modicum of predictability and routine, allows life to make sense to the person living it.

(King et al., 2016, p. 212)

Existential approaches to meaning, such as that of logotherapy, Viktor Frankl's (1985) Model of Existential Therapy, state that we experience meaning in life not just because of a belief that there is intrinsic meaning, but also because we can choose to respond to life in a responsible and self-transcendent manner. Frankl's meaning-seeking idea is about how to live with courage, freedom and responsibility (Wong, 2014).

Coaches can help their clients to explore meaning from multiple perspectives:

- Deriving meaning from daily tasks, such as domestic chores that enhance one's life or those of others, and could be perceived as a token of love
- Meaning and purpose as a calling in life
- Meaning assigned to living life according to one's values.

Accomplishment

Accomplishment relates to completing something, achieving a goal, or conquering a milestone. It is about experiencing satisfaction with our progress and development. Although this dimension can be directly linked to goals and outcomes, there are other perspectives to be considered. Exploring clients' views on accomplishment as a concept can shed light on their *experience of living* and help them expand their awareness of daily experiences that can be perceived as 'accomplishments'. An example of a client who lives with a long-term health condition comes to mind. When using the PERMA framework for coaching this client, he could not think of anything that he had accomplished over a considerable period of time, as he was recovering from a spell in hospital and '*had not been able to do much*' (his words) since getting back home. The coaching helped him identify the steps he was taking towards his recovery and consider how he was improving progressively, for example, getting out of bed in the morning, cooking a healthy meal, or finding the energy to chat to a neighbour. Because he took these things for granted before his illness, he did not see them as accomplishments per se, and the coaching helped him reframe these achievements and derive a sense of pride and satisfaction in his recovery, no longer dismissing these daily experiences.

Case study: Wellbeing in teams: coaching with PERMA

The PERMA model can be helpful when working with teams in organisations. The structured nature of this model means that the coach can work through the various aspects of the model with the clients, using coaching questions to

Figure 3.3 The PERMA Wellbeing Model

Positive emotions
(positive emotions, feeling joy, hope and contentment)

Engagement
(feeling involved, focused and motivated)

Relationships
(feeling connected and supported)

Meaning
(feeling valued; knowing your contribution)

Achievement
(feeling capable and accomplished)

Source: Adapted from Seligman (2012).

elicit reflections and discussions, and encouraging both individual as well as collective accountability.

In an organisational setting, it is important to consider the elements of PERMA from both an individual perspective and from a collective perspective. Working with teams can be incredibly helpful in exploring team practices that can be changed to the benefit of individuals and the team. To illustrate how this works in practice, I will use a case study of a media team of five who, during the COVID-19 pandemic, commissioned a team coaching programme to support them with wellbeing. The team lead did not have specific goals to tackle during the coaching programme, but the coach noticed that some team members seemed less engaged and that the team lead felt her energy levels dipping, experiencing low mood and motivation as a result. During the course of five 90-minute sessions delivered fortnightly, the team went through the different aspects of PERMA. The coaching programme itself served as a catalyst for team cohesion and supported the relational needs of the team. The protected reflective space was used for support, which was something completely different from the day-to-day, mostly transactional and performance-led interactions the team was used to having.

The coaching explored individuals' experiences, collective impact and accountability, with a pragmatic and solution-focused approach, reflected in the following questions for each aspect of the PERMA model (Figure 3.3):

- What can you, as an individual, do to support yourself in this area?
- What can you do to support others?
- What are the working practices serving as barriers and enablers in this area?
- What can the team do collectively to improve in this area?

Positive psychology interventions

As mentioned in Chapter 2, positive psychology interventions (PPIs) are intentional activities or exercises that help us foster positive emotions, behaviours and thoughts. These can be used during a coaching session as an exercise, or given to the client to complete in between coaching sessions. Giving clients something to work on in between sessions can be helpful for several reasons.

First, it encourages reflection, which can improve self-awareness and understanding, both crucial to support change and personal growth. Second, it allows clients to experiment with different tools and strategies to see what suits them best. Third, it keeps the momentum going. Here are some PPIs to try with your clients.

- *Three good things*: This is a simple exercise. Each night, the client should reflect on their day and write down three things that went well and why (reflecting on their role in it going positively). They don't need to be big things but something that made the person feel grateful, proud, happy, hopeful, and relaxed. Just a sentence or two is sufficient, but the client can write as much as they want. This exercise helps people counteract the negativity bias and realise that, no matter what, good things do happen every day.
- *Best possible self*: This is a writing exercise that asks the client to consider what their life would be like in the future if things go as well as they can. They should think about all the various aspects of their life: personal, professional, social, and visualise in as much detail as possible (including seeing, hearing, and feeling). When a clear visualisation materialises, the details should be written down in a very specific way.
- *Savouring*: This is about appreciating and being fully present and aware of positive experiences in our lives. Sometimes it is easy to lose sight of the positive moments and experiences we have in our lives. For example, when we go on holiday or when we are more relaxed, we notice things around us much more; our experience has more vibrancy, texture and colour. We are more consciously aware of our positive feelings and experiences, which may not be the case when we are rushing out of the door to go to work, preoccupied with the health of a loved one or worried about whether we will complete a project within the deadline.

There are three types of savouring experiences (Smith & Bryant, 2017):

- Savouring the past, or reminiscing
- Savouring the present
- Savouring the future or anticipation.

They can also be focused internally, for example, feeling pride for winning a competition or externally, such as seeing the Northern Lights.

Research shows that there is a link between savouring and wellbeing. This can be explained by the positive feelings we experience when savouring these moments. Furthermore, our ability to direct our minds and experience can contribute to our sense of meaning and personal growth, especially if we are able 'to attend to and appreciate positive aspects of adversity, leading to positive emotions and eudaimonic well-being' (Smith & Bryant, 2017, p. 142).

A world of too much

A common scenario in my coaching practice is clients who feel overwhelmed by the demands of daily life; so much so that they find it hard to disconnect from work, social media, and technology. Some have great lives but they don't enjoy themselves because they find it difficult to just 'be'. They are in a constant state of hyper-vigilance, restlessness and distraction. They feel like spectators in their own lives.

It is so easy in the 'busyness' of our daily lives to either ignore the positive experiences and/or focus on what is not going so well. But there are many savouring strategies (Smith & Bryant, 2017) that can help us tip the (negative) balance, including:

- Sharing positive experiences with others
- Actively creating and building memories of positive experiences
- Acknowledging and celebrating our personal successes, however small
- Physically displaying positive experiences, such as laughing and hugging
- Being aware of the present moment and the positive experiences contained in that moment
- Counting our blessings.

Your client may think of other strategies or they may have their favoured methods of capturing their present and positive experiences, through photography, art, music, or writing. Being more present in our lives will not only improve how we perceive things but also help us to be more present during our experiences with others.

A savouring exercise is an invitation for us to step into that space in our lives by being fully present; it is a request for us to stop and pay attention, to enjoy the positive moments and experiences, no matter how fleeting. It is a warning sign against living on autopilot and a wake-up call to us all to live with intention.

Gratitude

Fostering feelings of gratitude is another great strategy to boost wellbeing (Lomas et al., 2014). The benefits of being grateful expand across many areas, from positive impact on our physical health, including better quality of sleep; emotional and social functioning; lowered stress and greater satisfaction with our romantic partner. Gratitude has been linked to positive emotions, altruism, trust, pro-social behaviour and social integration. There are some amazingly simple gratitude interventions we can share with our clients. These are easy for them to implement and, with so many benefits, gratitude exercises can facilitate some quick wins for clients and help them get into a more positive frame of mind. I have added some examples of such exercises in the Appendix: the Wellbeing Coach's Toolkit.

Reflections on wellbeing goals and outcomes

By its very nature, coaching is about supporting people to make changes in their lives and wellbeing coaching is no different. Goals have a significant role to play in the change process. However, given the complexity and multi-faceted nature of wellbeing, it is worth spending some time considering distinct types of goals and the importance of giving our clients enough time to explore their wellbeing, before helping them articulate goals to move them towards their desired wellbeing outcome. This will help them consider their individual needs and aspirations, as opposed to what other people or society may be telling them about wellbeing, as well as how they can get there.

Although SMART goals (**S**pecific; **M**easurable; **A**chievable; **R**elevant, and **T**ime-bound) may come to mind when we think about goals, not everyone benefits from this approach. Some will prefer to set goals that are broad and abstract. Emmons (1992) refers to them as so-called high-level strivers, while others prefer to frame their goals in more concrete, specific terms, he called them low-level strivers.

Let's explore the literature around goals to see how we can better support our clients.

What are goals?

Ordinarily speaking, a goal can be defined as a desired result. But it can be a lot more than that. Little (1989), for example, wrote about personal projects, which included actions ranging from 'the trivial pursuits of a typical Tuesday (e.g., "cleaning up my room") to the magnificent obsessions of a lifetime (e.g., "liberate my people")'. In wellbeing terms, our clients may be interested in multiple 'personal projects', in different areas of their lives involving varying degrees of complexity.

Goals can also be broken down into three categories: performance, behavioural and learning (Latham et al., 2016). A performance goal is focused more on the outcome than on the behaviour needed to achieve that outcome, although they can be linked. For example, someone's goal of running a marathon (performance goal) may involve a behavioural goal (exercising regularly) and a learning goal (understanding fitness). It is important to note that each of these types of goals will draw our attention to specific actions or outcomes: achieving (performance), doing (behaviours) and learning, all of which can impact motivation according to individuals' drivers for change. Another crucial factor is timing: goals can be defined to be achieved in the short, medium or long term, or a combination of these.

It is likely that a person's wellbeing goals will include a combination of several types of goals across different aspects of the person's life. Wellbeing is enhanced when individuals are engaged in personal projects that are meaningful, well-structured, supported by others, not unduly stressful, and which engender a sense of efficacy (Little, 1989). Coaches can help their clients to consider what the right approach is for them, and how to hit the sweet spot with regard to each enhancement. As Lucy's story at the beginning of this chapter illustrated, wellbeing is not something we improve by enlarging our to-do list.

Wellbeing: competing priorities

It is not unusual for clients to have various priorities, a few of which may conflict with one another. Typical examples are combining career aspirations with caring responsibilities, raising a family and developing other personal projects and ambitions.

We know that conflicting goals can adversely impact the client's ability to achieve their goals. In addition, conflicting goals can cause an internal tension and stress for clients, with a negative impact on their wellbeing. When clients seek help and when it becomes clear that they have far too many priorities to fit into those 24-hour days, one of the options is to work with them on their values. This can help with decision-making and action planning. Values can be used as a compass for the client when deciding on priorities and the resources and energy they will devote to these priorities. Although it is not always easy, getting clear on what is important can be liberating. For example, I worked with an executive in his fifties whose health was suffering due to the impact of long working hours. Although he recognised the challenges and knew 'what I have to do', he found it difficult to stick to his plans as work pressure took precedence over anything else in his life. On top of his health problems, he also felt disconnected from his family and friends. When we worked on his values, it became clear that his career was the most important thing in his life at that particular moment in time, as he felt he was within touching distance of getting his dream job. He found it difficult to admit that he was pushing his family down the priority ladder and recognised the stress this internal turmoil was causing him. He used coaching to devise a short- and medium-term plan for his career, to develop some healthier habits, and to engage in a more meaningful way with his family, so that the focus was on quality versus quantity. Having a clearer plan and developing a more honest relationship with himself and others around him had a positive impact on his life. The coaching programme lasted nine months.

Self-concordant goals

If we align our goals to our values, we feel more in tune with ourselves, which contributes to our wellbeing. Sheldon and Elliot's (1999) research showed that individuals make more progress towards self-concordant goals (aligned to their values). This is because we are more likely to put sustained effort into achieving these goals than goals that conflict with our values or are simply not as important to us. This is an interesting area of exploration for wellbeing coaches. Every day we are bombarded with messages about what we should and should not do to enhance our life experience and wellbeing. As expected, some clients will bring to coaching the goals they feel they 'ought to have' to improve their lives. There can be conflict between what clients want to do, what they think they ought to do and what they are told to do by others, such as family and friends, healthcare professionals, educators, and so on. We help them delve deeper to understand their innermost motivations and values.

Case study: Kevin's story

One of my clients, Kevin, saw his health, both physical and mental, deteriorate during the COVID-19 pandemic. He came to coaching through his company's wellbeing scheme, which included one-to-one coaching as part of their offer. At the first session, he told me everything he knew he should be doing but was not. He was disappointed in himself and highly self-critical. During the coaching programme, we uncovered his 'compelling reasons' for wanting to improve his wellbeing, which were directly or indirectly related to his value of 'contribution'. He worked on international projects and was passionately invested in the benefits his work, team and company brought to thousands of people worldwide. He was then able to align his efforts to fit with these com-pelling reasons and 'undo' the damage the pandemic had caused to his wellbeing, including its negative impact on daily habits, behaviours, thoughts and feelings. This increased his commitment and understanding of the real drivers for his motivation.

Kevin's case illustrate how sometimes – not always – clients are able to con-nect to the real reason behind the 'ought to' statements that make them feel disconnected from their purpose for wellbeing. By making the link between values and goals, they are back in self-concordant goals territory which is easier for them to navigate. Self-concordant goals are not always pleasurable: 'One might willingly pursue an objective from which one derives no experi-ential enjoyment if the unpleasant task is guided by mature, self-disciplined valuation and a sense of ownership of the goal' (Sheldon & Elliot, 1999, p. 484).

The types of goals and how our client defines them may play a key role in whether they have the volition not only to get started, but also to sustain their efforts to achieve what they want. Therefore, it is worth bearing in mind theories and research so that we can help our clients increase their chances of being successful. Goal-setting theory (Locke & Latham, 2002), which is based on decades of research and field studies, tells us that people are more likely to achieve harder and specific goals than easy, non-specific ones. The theory also suggests that bigger and complex goals should be broken down into smaller chunks to retain motivation. This makes sense if we consider self-efficacy the-ory (Bandura, 1997), which is an individual's belief in their capacity and ability to achieve specific goals. The more self-efficacy we experience, the higher our confidence levels will be. If our goal is complex and hard, breaking it down into smaller, tangible, and achievable sub-goals helps us develop self-efficacy and boosts our motivation. It also helps us manage expectations and calibrate

Figure 3.4 Self-efficacy helps the client to keep going

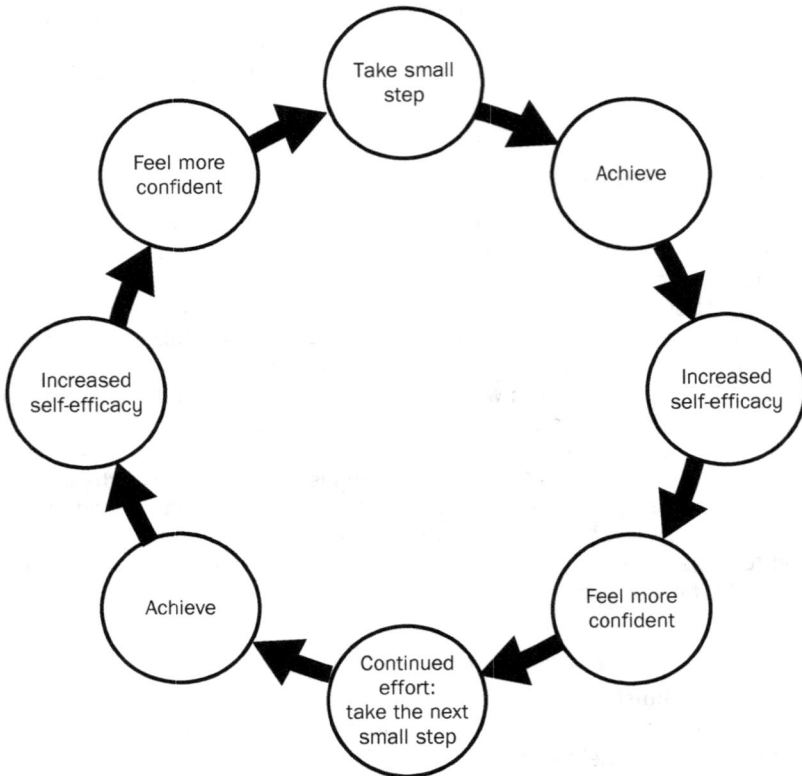

the amount of time and effort required. Each 'small' win increases our sense of self-efficacy and confidence, which in turn increases motivation concerning continuing our efforts towards the bigger goal.

According to the self-efficacy theory, the more we believe we can do something, the more we commit to taking the required actions towards achieving it and, as a result, the more likely it is to be achieved (Figure 3.4). For example, if you believe you can achieve high marks in a particular essay, you become more motivated to do what is necessary to do well. 'Unless people believe they can be successful in obtaining desired outcomes, they have little incentive to undertake activities or to persevere in the case of difficulties or failures' (Caprara et al., 2006, p. 32).

Micro-actions

Another similar idea that can be helpful for our clients is the idea of micro-actions – actions that require little time, effort and resources and, therefore, are easy to commit to on a regular basis. A study with 28 undergraduate students from the University of Kentucky showed that several micro-actions brought about positive macro-changes in participants' lives, including improved academic performance (Kim, 2014). These micro-actions included getting up 10–20 minutes earlier in the morning; putting the phone away during class; writing down plans and using assignment planners; briefly reviewing course material; and exercising.

Even the achievement of these small actions can boost the clients' sense of achievement and self-efficacy, which is encouraging for them. On top of that, achievements – however small – will boost positive emotions, and research shows that people feel positive emotions when they achieve their goals or make progress towards them (Snyder et al., 2002). Although there is no silver bullet when it comes to taking action and keeping our clients motivated, there are a few strategies that can be helpful. It may also be useful to include some micro-actions in day-to-day planning to keep our clients engaged and smiling.

Goal theory tells us that the crucial factors in goal attainment are commitment, ability to achieve and getting feedback on progress. 'So long as a person is committed to the goal, has the requisite ability to attain it, and does not have conflicting goals, there is a positive, linear relationship between goal difficulty and task performance' (Locke & Latham, 2006, p. 265).

Goals that fit into the 'ought to' category are not always at the top of our minds and may require extra effort to be completed. However, it is not always possible to discard these goals altogether as some of us will need to pursue them to improve our health and wellbeing. For example, some of us may really enjoy exercising while others not so much. Although we can think about different ways to exercise and try to work as much as possible with something that is positive, the excitement may still be lacking. A way to support clients with these types of goals is to help them understand their compelling reasons for wanting to achieve these goals and how they may align to their values, as Kevin's story shows. Sometimes we are fixated on the 'what' (the goal) and the fact that we are not inspired by it, whereas the key to find the commitment and energy to pursue the goal may be in the 'why'.

Motivation

Reflecting on several types of goals, finding the big 'why', and aligning to our values are all valuable steps to help our clients to understand what might work for them and explore the strategies they may need to put in place, not only to get started but, equally important, to keep going. A vision alone is not sufficient for us to create sustainable change. We need motivation.

Motivation is a vast area of study in its own right. This section will help you understand some of its basic principles. Some scholars have posited that there are three basic psychological needs that motivate us. These are autonomy, competence and relatedness, which are also the psychological needs that support people's wellbeing, according to Self-Determination Theory (Ryan & Deci, 2001). Autonomy is about knowing that we have the freedom to make our own choices. Competence is related to feeling that we can do something well, and relatedness is about being connected to others.

Self-determination theory is also interested in what drives people to choose their goals, which can be either intrinsic or extrinsic needs. Extrinsic motivation is associated with external rewards such as attractiveness, fame and doing better than others are, whereas intrinsic motivation comes from personal satisfaction or growth. Studies have found that intrinsic goals tend to be linked to higher levels of wellbeing, more autonomy and improved performance. In wellbeing pursuits, it is likely that clients may be motivated by both intrinsic and extrinsic goals. A good balance will help them achieve the outcomes they want.

Another factor that influences people's ability to achieve goals is their perceived locus of control, in other words, whether they feel empowered to make changes in their lives or not. Those with an internal locus of control see themselves as the primary determinants of what happens to them and those with an external locus of control see external factors, such as chance and powerful others, as the primary determinants of what happens to them (Rotter, 1966).

As expected, the degree to which you feel you have control of your circumstances will have a direct impact on how you feel about your personal goals and choices. It is always worth reflecting upon your views on personal choice and what is within your sphere of influence.

Although we want to work positively with our clients, it is important to understand that their motivation for wellbeing goals may also come from negative emotions, such as fear and frustration, and these can be powerful. For example, let's think about a health goal around 'becoming physically fitter'. First, we need to explore what that means for our clients. As we dig deeper into the client's compelling reason to want to become fitter, we may encounter the following explanations (Figure 3.5).

Figure 3.5 Types of motivation

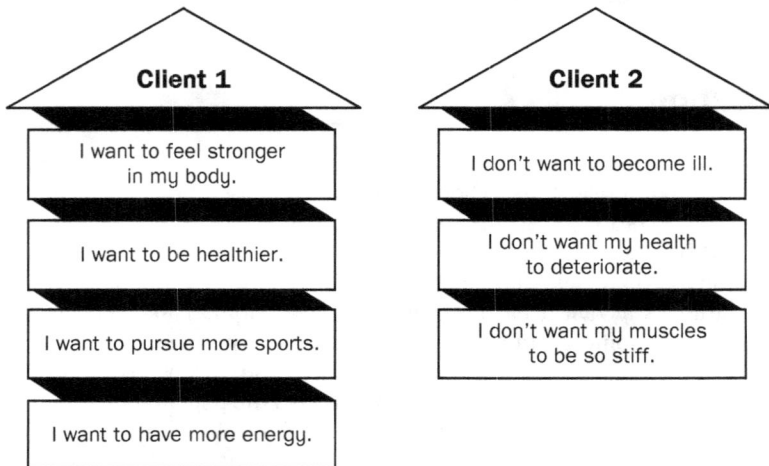

Client 1	Client 2
I want to feel stronger in my body.	I don't want to become ill.
I want to be healthier.	I don't want my health to deteriorate.
I want to pursue more sports.	I don't want my muscles to be so stiff.
I want to have more energy.	

There is a marked difference in these responses and they will influence your client's ability to commit to change and sustain it. When my clients say they want to embrace a healthier lifestyle, I often tell them the following scenario:

> It is wintertime. It is 6 o'clock in the morning and it is really cold and windy outside. What would persuade you to rise early? What is your compelling reason for leaving your warm bed to pursue your fitness goal?

Someone whose motivation to exercise is to feel healthy will have a totally different internal dialogue on this said winter's day than the person who does not want to be ill – and both are equally valid. Helping your client to connect with their compelling reason(s) is very important as that compelling reason has the power to propel them. This may well be a simplistic way of looking at motivation and many of us will experience both types of motivation – towards (something we want) and away from (something we don't want), but it does work.

When your client is able to articulate simply and clearly *the big why* for wanting the things they want for themselves, they find something powerful to connect to when the going gets tough, as inevitably it will, in the process of creating change. Moreover, like the work on values, it helps them sift through the narratives they have in their heads and understand what is truly important to them as opposed to what they have been told should be important.

Research corner: coaching for wellbeing

While there is a vast array of theories and practices that coaches can apply to support clients' wellbeing, the same cannot be said for empirical studies in coaching for wellbeing as a specific coaching modality. Only a few research studies were specifically designed to explore the impact of coaching on wellbeing of individuals. In saying that, there have been many studies in which researchers noted the positive impact of coaching on people's wellbeing as an associated beneficial outcome, even when wellbeing was not a direct focus of the coaching intervention.

For example, in 2003 Grant conducted an empirical study where 20 graduate students participated in a group life coaching intervention based on solution-focused therapy. The results showed that participants' mental health and quality of life improved (Grant, 2003). Another example is a study conducted by Linley et al. (2010), which was designed to test how a coaching strengths model can help goal progression. The results showed an increase in participants' wellbeing. In other research, Green and colleagues (2014) compared the effectiveness of a cognitive-behavioural solution-focused coaching intervention and a positive psychology intervention. Both coaching approaches were found to have the potential to contribute to wellbeing.

A study on the impact of personal systems coaching on self-efficacy, goals achievement and the wellbeing of Israeli single mothers (Bar, 2014) showed a statistically significant increase in life satisfaction and self-efficacy, two constructs closely associated with wellbeing.

It is important to note how these studies explore some of the theoretical underpinnings of coaching for wellbeing, such as the importance of self-concordant goals, and the role of self-efficacy and goal achievement in life satisfaction, for example.

Few studies focus exclusively on increasing the clients' wellbeing from the outset. One such study is that of Davis (2015), which examined how coaching influenced employee wellbeing, organisational culture and productivity. Their findings pointed to a 'connection between the coaching process and personal feelings of wellbeing' (p. 247). Some participants linked wellbeing directly to the coaching they received, while for others the 'connection between coaching and well-being was expressed as more of an indirect relationship in which coaching could improve performance and achievement at work, or could yield a greater sense of perspective, which, in turn, caused feelings of well-being to increase' (pp. 247–248).

In my own study, which I will explore fully in Chapters 6 and 7, I developed a group coaching model that has helped improve the wellbeing of individuals. The model can be used both in group and individual coaching and was based on wellbeing theories and available empirical evidence.

4 Fostering long-lasting changes

Readiness for lifestyle change

Sustainable change takes time. Think of when you tried to alter something in your life. Perhaps you tried to form a new habit. You make a decision, set a goal and a date to get started. On the first day, you are strong, resolute, and determined. On the second day, you are feeling good about your decision. By day three or four, you are not feeling so strong. You manage to keep going, but by day five, your mind chatter is working overtime to find excuses for you not to engage with whatever it is that you were so keen to bring into your life. You tell yourself that it did not work this time, but you will definitely start again next week. The following week, you may start over, or decide to wait another week, fortnight, month, and so on.

Gym membership statistics demonstrate this pattern. Every December, many people promise themselves that, after indulging and treating themselves over the festive season, they will join the gym in January and get into a much healthier way of life by exercising more and eating healthily. So, come the 1st January they go to their local gym, sign up, get kitted out in new trainers and workout gear, and off they go. But not for long. According to IHRSA, the Global Health and Fitness Association, 12 per cent of new members join the gym in January; 4 per cent of these new members will have already quit by the end of January; 14 per cent by the end of February and 50 per cent will have quit within six months.

We have all been there, but what can we do to make changes that are sustainable and/or reduce the risks of 'falling off the wagon'? According to the Transtheoretical Model of Change (DiClemente & Prochaska, 1998), we do not change behaviour quickly, but need to go through six stages, in a cyclical way, and the likelihood is that we will, more often than not, 'relapse' before being fully able to maintain the change for six months or longer.

The model was originally developed as a framework for substance abuse interventions, but it can be especially useful for coaches working with clients who want to stop negative habits and effect positive changes in their lives. The model not only helps us understand the distinct stages of change, but also explains the processes that can help clients progress through them. Moreover, by predicting that there will be challenges and 'relapses' ahead, we can help our clients to better prepare for them, so that, when they do occur, they can quickly get back on track.

Stages of change

The six stages of change are: (1) precontemplation; (2) contemplation; (3) preparation; (4) action; (5) maintenance; and (6) termination:

1 *Precontemplation*: During this stage the client is exploring their options and they have no intention to take action. They may even be unaware that their behaviour is having a negative impact on their lives and the lives of those around them.
2 *Contemplation* (plan to take action within six months): They have noticed that the behaviour is having an impact and they are beginning to contemplate changing it. They may be weighing up the pros and cons of the behaviour, and perhaps considering how it fits into their lives and the patterns they have created. They may still feel ambivalent about changing.
3 *Preparation* (plan to take action within 30 days): They are getting ready to take action; they can see the benefits of changing their behaviour and there is a sense of momentum for change to happen.
4 *Action* (made the change less than six months ago): First steps are taken towards the change and the client feels good about it. They are excited about the healthier lifestyle they are creating for themselves.
5 *Maintenance* (kept the change for at least six months): Client is able to maintain the change. They work hard to prevent relapse, which they experienced in earlier stages.
6 *Termination*: This stage was not part of the original model; people achieving this stage have no desire to go back to their previous unhealthy ways and feel confident they can maintain the new behaviour without relapsing.

The good news is that, once we reach the maintenance stage, we are more likely to keep up with the change and eventually get to the termination stage, in which the change no longer needs conscious effort on our part to maintain it. The not-so-good news is that most of us will relapse during these stages and will have to go back to the beginning. Although it would be great to be able to go from contemplation to termination in a linear way, change is not linear and it will require consistent effort.

The idealised change looks like Figure 4.1.

But the change in real life looks like Figure 4.2.

To progress through these stages, we use ten processes of change, which include cognitive, affective, and evaluative strategies to support us through the change. These processes are:

Figure 4.1 Idealised change

A ────────────▶ B

Figure 4.2 The spiral of change

1 *Consciousness-raising*: Becoming aware of wanting to change and the positive impact of desired change.

2 *Dramatic relief*: Tuning into our emotions about the change we want to make and/or the current (less desirable) behaviour.

3 *Self-re-evaluation*: Imagine ourselves as the person who has made the changes; associate the changes with who we want to be.

4 *Environmental re-evaluation*: Realise the impact of our negative behaviour on others.

5 *Social-liberation*: Notice that others validate and support the change.

6 *Self-liberation*: commitment to change by knowing we can change (self-efficacy).

7 *Helping relationships*: Having a network of people who can support us through change.

8 *Counter-conditioning*: Substituting healthy behaviours and thoughts for unhealthy behaviours and thoughts.

9 *Reinforcement management*: Rewarding our successes.

10 *Stimulus control*: Remove reminders in our environment of the behaviour we want to eliminate.

Although all these processes are helpful throughout the change cycle, some can be particularly relevant to specific stages. Consciousness-raising is important in the contemplation stages and into the action stage; self-re-evaluation, self-liberation, helping relationships, and reinforcement management are important during the action stage; and counter-conditioning and stimulus control are important in the maintenance stage. DiClemente and Prochaska (1998)

Table 4.1 The processes of change

Contemplation	Action	Maintenance
Awareness-raising	Awareness-raising	Counter-conditioning
	Self-re-evaluation	Stimulus control
	Self-liberation	
	Helping relationships	
	Reinforcement management	

state that by using these processes at the right time, i.e., the stage the client is experiencing, increases the client's chances of succeeding (Table 4.1).

This model emphasises the client's ability to recognise that they have the autonomy to change and that they can change. Self-efficacy is important and so is building an image of self that is aligned with the changes they want to make. For example, if we stick to the gym example, clients who want to build a habit of going to the gym on a regular basis need to see themselves as 'gym-goers'. They also need to believe they can exercise and achieve their fitness goals. If they don't, the likelihood is that they will themselves undermine their attempts to create new behaviour.

It also leverages the importance of values, especially in the self-re-evaluation process, including an 'assessment of which values clients will try to actualize, to act on, and to make real. Clients also need to assess which values they will let die' (DiClemente & Prochaska, 1998, p. 9). The client's self-concept can be one of the greatest barriers they need to overcome in order to change. In well-being coaching, it is often the case that clients want to create the ever-elusive 'work–life balance'. I prefer to call it only 'life balance' as work is part of life as opposed to separate from it. In any case, clients who are struggling to switch off from work or who are working more than they would like to may come to coaching to try to create a more balanced life. Here are some examples of how people's self–concept may jeopardise their efforts to work less:

- They see themselves as indispensable and therefore take on everything that comes their way.
- They try to be super-efficient and therefore work longer hours to complete tasks instead of negotiating deadlines, delegating or asking for help.
- They are perfectionists and find it hard to settle for *good enough.*
- They worry that they are not good enough and overcompensate by working harder.

Clients experiencing the above may find it more difficult to say 'no' to work and create healthy boundaries. The self-re-evaluation process can help them look at their values and their identity, and change how they see themselves, before moving on to making changes. Like the example of 'seeing oneself as a gym-goer', in this case, the client needs to see themselves as someone whose work does not dominate their lives and/or someone who has a full, satisfying life outside work, or any other helpful self-concepts.

Applying the model in coaching

First, it is helpful to identify which stage your client is at in relation to the changes they want to make and assess their readiness. Knowing that most people in the early stages of change will feel ambivalent and helping them strengthen their commitment by working with values, understanding their motivation and helping them get crystal clear on their compelling reason, are all helpful coaching strategies. Coaches can also use the processes explained above during the various stages of change.

A tool that is particularly useful to help clients explore the impact of changing versus staying the same is the decision balance sheet (Janis & Mann, 1977), which can be relevant in the initial stages of the change process (Table 4.2). This is a simple tool to use. You ask your client to list as many benefits and as many disadvantages of changing and of staying the same as they can think of. Sometimes, clients struggle to think of the benefits of a behaviour they see as negative but the reality is that there are advantages to those behaviours – perhaps they are just not aware of them yet.

In the example above about a client striving to achieve a more fulfilling life balance, the benefits of continuing working excessively could be: recognition from peers and managers of being effective and efficient; compliments received for the high-standard of the work produced; being seen as the person who is loyal and always available; and external validation received which counteracts low self-esteem. All of these give the person a sense of professional accomplishment and satisfaction. The downside could include less quality time with family and friends, burnout, stress, anxiety, and lack of self-care.

If they change the existing pattern, the disadvantages could be that both peers and the manager may notice the change and will have to recalibrate their expectations; the client will need to have difficult conversations to negotiate

Table 4.2 The decision balance sheet

	Changing	Staying the same
Benefits		
Disadvantages		

more achievable goals and deadlines; and they may need to lower their own expectations and reconsider their priorities. On the upside, they will have more head space to connect with people outside of work and with other pleasurable activities; they will increase their level of self-care, which can have a positive impact on their physical and mental health; and they will feel less stressed and less anxious.

These are not exhaustive lists, just examples to illustrate how the decision balance tool can be used to put things into perspective. The tool will help with the awareness-raising process, and the coach can use any other coaching tools and techniques to support the other processes.

Although it may be tempting to want to get our clients into action mode as quickly as possible, this model calls for a more measured approach. Quickly getting into action does not translate into quickly getting to maintenance (termination) stage. In fact, by working through the stages and the processes, we will ensure that the client has gained insight into their strengths that will propel them forward as well as the pitfalls for which they need to watch out. Moreover, as part of the coaching process, we can help clients to have their strategies ready for when they fall off the wagon, which can be followed by negative emotions, such as shame and guilt. The quicker they get back on track, the better and more likely they are to continue with their efforts, without losing momentum. Self-compassion exercises may support your client during tough times. Self-compassion is about giving ourselves the same kindness, care, and compassion that we would give to others. A simple way to think about self-compassion is to ask yourself: 'What would you say to your best friend/loved one in this situation?' Now say the same words to yourself. Research shows that self-compassion can improve emotional resilience, self-esteem, and reduce stress and anxiety (Neff, 2011). You will find a few self-compassion exercises in the Appendix: Wellbeing Coach's Toolkit at the end of the book.

Encourage your client to prepare as much as possible for the maintenance stage and assess what will help keep them going, such as positive reinforcement, rewards and keeping away from people and/or circumstances that could negatively impact their efforts.

Long-lasting habits

When we achieve the last stage (termination), we can maintain our new behaviours without much effort as they become part of our daily lives. Forming a new habit can take time. Research found that the average time it takes to form a new habit is 66 days, with individual times varying from 18 to 254 days (Lally et al., 2010). With that in mind, when clients want to achieve long-lasting lifestyle changes, it is useful to know that it can take a while. This helps them manage their own expectations, as well as using the coaching process to maximise their chances of success. If they want to stop doing something that they perceive to be negative, such as overworking, research shows that they can maximise their changes by forming a new habit instead, which is called behavioural replacement, part of the counter-conditioning process in the trans-theoretical model. For example, clients may decide to improve their exercise routine and use that to stop working at a particular time, or they can take up a new hobby or activity.

People's wellbeing vision is likely to include long-term goals and lifestyle changes and they may well have mixed feelings concerning short-term gain and long-term benefit. For example, have an extra 15 minutes in bed in the morning (short-term gain), instead of getting up and preparing a healthy break-fast or engaging in reflection/meditation and feeling healthier both physically and mentally (long-term benefit). Creating good habits can be instrumental in helping people achieve the lifestyle changes they desire. Habits are formed through consistent repetition of behaviour (Lally et al., 2010). Other factors include:

- Is the behaviour rewarding?
- Is it easy or difficult? Easier behaviours are easier to embed.
- What are the obstacles? Have they been removed?
- Are there cues in the environment that serve as triggers for the behaviour?
- What are the motivation levels?

Preparing for change

Considering the multi-faceted nature of wellbeing and the challenges we all face when striving to create our 'wellbeing jigsaw', preparation for these changes will be key. Many coaching models and theories have 'action' as a key mechanism to effect change.

The nature of habit formation, as described above, and the fact that we can use good habits to scaffold our wellbeing vision and lifestyle mean that clients are more likely to do well if they choose their actions carefully and prepare for the changes they want to implement. Small actions that could help to build those habits that will support long-lasting change can become crucial to increase the client's chances of success. For example, if the client starts with adopting minor changes, such as short mindfulness exercises, moments of joy or the three good things exercise, they can slowly build a solid foundation for future changes. Moreover, as clients increase their sense of self-awareness, they are then able to create more effective strategies to sustain change and manage lapses.

Practical steps

In the Appendix: the Wellbeing Coach's Toolkit at the end of this book, you will find a Wellbeing Plan, which you can adapt to the needs of your clients.

Other considerations for the plan are shown in Table 4.3.

Table 4.3   Wellbeing plan

Goals	Action	Remember
Mix different types of goals, easy goals and stretch goals (more challenging); short-term and long-term	Consider including micro-actions in your wellbeing plan, e.g., three-minute mindfulness exercise, doing star jumps while you are waiting for the kettle to boil for your tea	Your compelling reason(s) and your vision
Chunk goals down to sub-goals	Put in place environmental cues that support the behaviour you want and remove cues that trigger behaviours you want to stop, i.e., if you want to eat healthily, put a bowl of fruit and healthy snacks in visible places and hide the 'treats' you don't want to eat	Be kind to yourself when the plan doesn't work and get back to it as quickly as you can
Self-concordant goals	Make the steps to take action as few and easy as possible, i.e., leave your gym gear visible with your trainers by the door; leave the musical instrument you want to learn in reach (not hidden in a cupboard somewhere in the house)	Build a support network of people who will encourage you along the way
	Create a routine, and practise being flexible with it, i.e., if you took up painting to get into flow and have booked time in your diary Mondays and Thursday evenings for it, be prepared to adapt if things get in the way	Be flexible
	'Tag' a new habit onto an existing on, i.e., if you have a cup of tea mid-morning, do a three-minute mindfulness exercise at the same time	Take your time
	Build your practice slowly: consistency and frequency are key	Do less, be more
		Enjoy: wellbeing is a journey, not a destination

Case study: Joanna's story

I worked with Joanna for eight months on an individual basis. Joanna is a 42-year-old HIV-positive woman with a low viral load, which means her illness is as controlled as it can be. She was feeling unhappy and felt she was lacking 'zest in life'. Since her diagnosis seven years ago, she went through challenging experiences in all aspects of her life. She left her job as she didn't feel able to work at the same pace and she didn't want to tell her employer about being HIV positive for fear of being stigmatised. She had had on–off relationships over the years and was now ready for a more committed long-term partnership. She had also distanced herself from her family and her parents did not know she was HIV positive. Her vision for wellbeing had her health at the centre with relationships, finding meaningful work and reconnecting with her family as priorities. At the beginning of the coaching programme, it became apparent that Joanna was overly critical of herself. Her internal dialogue was mostly negative and she found it difficult to self-regulate. To start with, I suggested she worked with self-compassion using mindfulness and CBT-informed exercises. Over the first few months of coaching, she built a straightforward easy-to-achieve 'five-a-day for her mind' routine, which she varied during the week. We worked very slowly, adding one thing at a time and trying and testing different activities and positive psychology interventions. She felt accomplished as she managed to create and embed a routine that felt right for her, and which was flexible and creative. She felt more confident to start exploring work options and took a volunteering position at a local charity. She also joined a dance class, which was 'the scariest thing I've ever done', but which not only connected her to the joy of dancing (and brought more zest to her life) but also connected her to a group of local people with similar interests.

5 | Becoming a wellbeing coach

In this chapter, I will address some of the professional challenges facing coaches working in these areas, including ethical practice, boundaries of coaching, and self-care.

The case for compassionate detachment

Compassion is important in coaching for many reasons. First, it allows us to care for our clients. 'It is characterised by feelings of warmth, concern and care for the other, as well as a strong motivation to improve the other's wellbeing. Compassion is feeling *for* and not feeling *with* the other' (Singer & Klimecki, 2014, p. R875). This is different from empathy, which is about sharing the feelings of others. As humans, we have the capacity to resonate with other people's feelings – we feel 'with them'. Second, it allows us to care for ourselves by helping us avoid empathic distress, which can lead to burnout and the avoidance of prosocial behaviours. Research shows that people who feel compassion are more likely to help than those who suffer from empathic distress.

Depending on the context in which we practise coaching and our own subjective experiences, we may be more or less vulnerable to empathic distress. But the advantage of practising compassionate detachment goes beyond that. What do I mean by detachment? Separating our clients' achievements or otherwise from our self-concept as coaches. For this to happen, we have to dial up our unconditional positive regard for our clients, and truly let them take responsibility and accountability for their choices and actions.

In wellbeing, this can be even more fraught with challenges, as we encounter clients whom we may perceive as positively contributing to their ill-being. On such occasions, the misconstrued mantra 'thou shall not be judgemental' can bring up some interesting internal tensions and dilemmas. As we all judge, our ability to bracket those judgements, self-regulate and get out of the way is what we endeavour to do when supporting our clients. Judging is what our brains do all the time; it is how we process and store information, how we make sense of the world, how we interact with people, how we get it right and how we get it wrong.

Back to compassionate detachment, the more 'detached' we are from our clients' choices and whether they achieve their goals, the more present we are as their thinking partners. This does not mean we will be colluding with them either. Challenging, facilitating insight and awareness are crucial.

You may think that your client is not looking after themselves enough; maybe they are stressed, overworked, and unfulfilled. They are seeking coaching potentially because they want to make changes, but the changes they want to make may not be the ones you expect. And you judge them. That's when compassionate detachment can be helpful as it helps you keep your agenda out of your client's way and fully engage with them where they are. Reminding ourselves of the multi-faceted and multi-layered nature of wellbeing can be helpful.

Mental health and wellbeing

In recent years, there has been increased effort to raise awareness of mental health issues and reduce the stigma of those experiencing mental illness. A large number of people will experience mental health issues in their lifetime and/or know someone who has these issues. The World Health Organization estimates that 1 in 8 people lives with a mental disorder, with a high prevalence of depression and anxiety. Considering such statistics, it is likely that coaches will be working with clients who are experiencing mental health issues, including coaches focusing on wellbeing. In fact, a key part of the work that we do may be around supporting individuals to develop positive mental health, and organisations to enable such development.

The challenges for professional coaches are many, including considerations about the boundaries of their practice, the understanding of mental illness, and ethical implications of our professional decisions. These are complex issues with no easy solution. This section will explore some of the issues and raise points for reflection.

Understanding mental illness

Coaches are not trained to diagnose or treat mental illness. As such, we are advised to signpost our clients to more appropriate and suitable services, if we think their needs will be better met by other professionals, including therapists and doctors.

Improving our understanding of mental health conditions can support us in our ability to make informed decisions and to work in partnership with our clients and discuss their psychological distress. I would highly recommend that those interested in supporting people's mental wellbeing also consider deepening their understanding of mental distress. A starting point is completing Mental Health First Aid training. 'Concerns relating to coaches' abilities to recognise mental health problems and manage them effectively have been expressed in various studies (Hart, Blattner, & Leipsic, 2001; Grant & Zackon, 2004; Turner, 2010; Jinks, 2010)' (Bachkirova & Baker, 2018, p. 488).

It is also important to bear in mind that mental health diagnosis is never value-free and is embedded in a cultural and socio-economic context. For example, until 1973, homosexuality was listed in the *Diagnostic and Statistical Manual of Mental Disorders* (DSM) as a mental illness.

Furthermore, according to the National Institute of Health and Care Excellence, some mental health illness, such as depression and anxiety, can be experienced on a scale from mild and moderate to severe. This will affect people's experience of symptoms such as feeling stressed, low, anxious, or worried, for example, which of course are also part of everyday experience for many of us.

Building a strong relationship with our clients, with a high level of trust and understanding, is vital to create a safe space for clients to share freely, without fear of being judged or misunderstood. The coach's ability to 'sit with' potentially difficult conversations on mental illness is also important. Remembering our role as coaches can be helpful.

Professional guidance for coaches, coming from the various codes of ethics and practice, such as the International Coaching Federation Code of Ethics and the Global Code of Ethics, agrees that coaches should signpost clients to more suitable services when their needs are beyond the remit of coaching. In practice, research shows that the boundaries between coaching and counselling are often blurred (Bachkirova & Baker, 2018) and some argue that there is a grey area where coaching and psychotherapeutic practices become undifferentiated (Bishop et al., 2018).

The severity and frequency of symptoms or behaviours may serve as an indication of when the client may need to access a different type of support (see Box 5.1 on crisis support and Box 5.2 on signs of mental health issues).

Dimensions of mental health

Using a dimensional approach to mental health and mental distress, which recognises the fluidity of our mental landscape, can give coaches an indication of areas of practice for both coaching and therapy, while acknowledging the blurred lines between these areas. Some scholars state that mental health is situated on a continuum; a study by Griffiths and Campbell (2008) indicated that clients were not situated in either coaching or counselling but fluctuated on a continuum between the two approaches (Figure 5.1).

It is not always easy for coaches to identify where clients may be on the mental health continuum and it is reasonable to expect some clients to mask their emotional state, especially if they believe there is a risk of repercussions on their professional lives, for example. The framework above can be used as a useful basis for reflection, with some reservations regarding the language used, such as categorical diagnosis and 'personal point of referral'. As mentioned previously, mental illness diagnosis is not value-free and mental health practitioners themselves may disagree on the diagnosis for a particular patient. Second, depending on the context, a referral is understood to be a formal written request to another professional asking them to see a client. In settings where coaching services are offered alongside therapy or counselling, this may well be the case. Otherwise, when there is a concern about the client's mental health condition, coaches will encourage their clients to seek medical or psychological advice. In the true spirit of coaching, as a partnership of equals in which the client is firmly in the driving seat, coaches will support their clients in taking steps towards getting further help.

Figure 5.1 The mental health and mental distress range

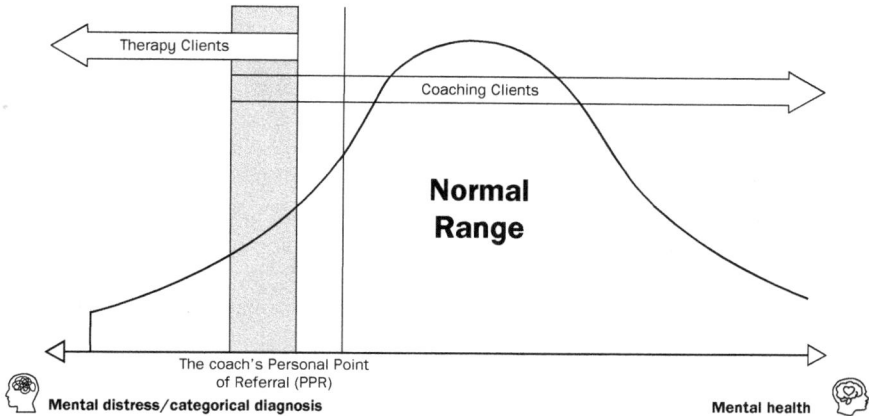

Source: Adapted from Cavanagh & Buckley (2014).

5.1 Crisis support

The International Coaching Federation lists anxiety, depression, eating disorders, post-traumatic stress, substance abuse, suicidal ideation, and thought disorders as issues where coaches should consider making a referral.

The only exception is when coaches believe the client to be in immediate risk of danger, either to themselves or to others. In such situations, the key consideration is safeguarding your client and/or others. The International Coaching Federation advises the following in crises:

- Call your local emergency number.
- Stay with the person until help arrives.
- Ask what means they have that may cause harm.
- Listen, but do not judge, argue, threaten, or yell. If you think someone is considering suicide, get help from a crisis or suicide prevention hotline.

Each country and locality will have their organisations offering support to those at risk. Here are organisations working worldwide:

- International Suicide Prevention Wiki: http://suicideprevention.wikia.com/wiki/International
- Befrienders Worldwide: https://www.befrienders.org/
- International Association for Suicide Prevention: https://www.iasp.info/resources/Crisis_Centres

Source: https://coachingfederation.org/app/uploads/2021/01/ClientReferral.pdf

5.2   Signs of mental health issues

These are just indicators. An assessment by a mental health specialist is required to confirm any diagnosis, in line with the *Diagnostic and Statistical Manual of Mental Disorders*, which is used by professionals as a guide for psychiatric diagnoses and treatment. Many of these signs, when seen in isolation, are part of what is considered normal behaviour.

- *Appearance*: Have you noticed a marked difference in the client's appearance and level of personal care? Is there anything unusual about their body language?
- *Behaviour*: Does the client appear agitated or nervous? Does the client's behaviour appear incoherent?
- *Mood*: Is the client demonstrating extreme emotions, either positive or negative? Are they unrelated to the context they are describing? Is the client apathetic?
- *Thoughts*: Is the client fixated on particular thoughts? Does the client appear irrational or deluded?
- *Intellect*: Have you noticed changes in the client's intellect over time?
- *Perception*: Is the client showing signs of experiencing the world in an unusual way?
- *Insight*: Does the client offer an explanation for these unusual signs? Does the explanation seem reasonable?

Source: Adapted from Cavanagh & Buckley (2014).

Professional responsibility

Coaches have a moral, ethical and professional obligation to be clear about the limitations of their professional training and experience, and contract with their clients accordingly. It is important to explain to clients the remit of your work as a wellbeing coach, as well as its limitations.

If the client is going through mental health issues, the options for client and coach are to delay, continue or stop the coaching programme. Although coaching can be used in parallel with other interventions, client and coach must consider the implications of this option, especially if it could interfere with other treatments or put the client under undue stress or pressure.

The role of supervision

Coaching supervision is important for all coaches and an essential part of keeping a professional coaching practice. As shown in the issues discussed in this chapter, coaching for wellbeing can bring some challenges. Supervision is a helpful resource for coaches who need guidance dealing with difficult issues and/or want to discuss the boundaries of their practice and questions around mental health.

Supervisors can fulfil a number of roles, including a developmental role, a normative role and a restorative role (Clutterbuck, Whitaker & Lucas, 2016). In the developmental role, supervisors help coaches 'grow their sense of mastery in their profession' (p. 122). In this role, the supervisor helps the coach develop skills, and gain knowledge, insights and perspectives. The normative role of the supervisor supports the coach in navigating ethical complexities in the contexts in which they are practising. In the restorative role, the supervisor supports the coach in their ability to practise. Here is where coaches discuss thoughts and feelings about their practice, careful to ensure they are fit to practise. Coaching can be as rewarding as it can be exhausting. Depending on the context, the clients, and the issues they bring to coaching, you will need to ensure that you have a good self-care routine and coaching processes that enable you to work at your best.

Organisations that decide to develop in-house coaching for wellbeing need to be mindful of ensuring that boundaries and confidentiality issues are clear and that there are robust processes in place to support both coaches and their clients. Capacity is also a critical point to consider. Coaching can be demanding and there will be a maximum number of clients that coaches will be able to assist at any given time.

5.3 Reflecting on signs of psychological distress

Coaches can use the following to guide their thinking in relation to clients who are showing signs of psychological distress:

- How long has the client's distress or dysfunction been going on?
- How extreme are the behaviours or responses (emotional, cognitive, or physiological) of the client?
- How pervasive are the distresses and patterns of dysfunctional behaviour? (Does the problem occur in one or multiple areas of the person's life, at one time or multiple times?)
- How defensive is the person? Does the person actively seek to avoid addressing the unhelpful behaviours? Do they deny the existence of problems in the face of considerable evidence to the contrary? Do they become overly aggressive, defensive or passive when appropriately challenged by the coach?

Considering further support from clinicians and other mental health professionals will be useful in some cases. The coach can open up the conversation about the client's needs and what help is available to them.

Source: Buckley (2010).

Encouraging positive mental health

The absence of mental illness does not necessarily equate to mental health and clients who have no diagnosable mental illness may experience low states of

Figure 5.2 The mental health continuum

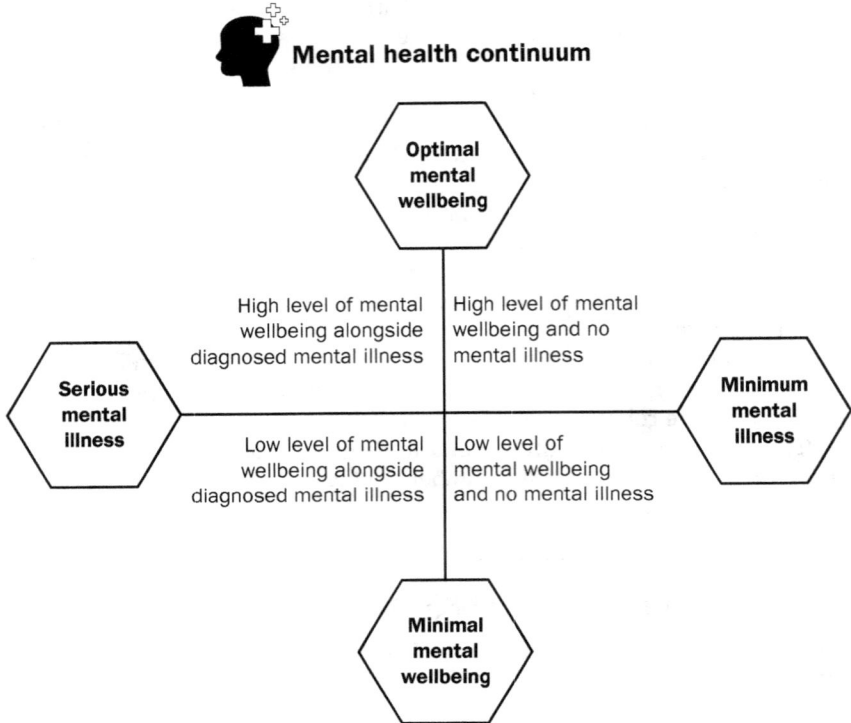

Source: Adapted from Slade (2010).

mental wellbeing. Individuals move along the mental health continuum depending on personal circumstances (Figure 5.2).

There are a number of mental wellbeing theories. One of them was developed by American sociologist and psychologist Corey Keyes, who coined the term 'flourishing'. Keyes' (2002) research showed that flourishing individuals function markedly better than languishing ones, reporting higher levels of functional goals, resilience, intimacy and low levels of helplessness.

Flourishing individuals have a high level of emotional, psychological and social wellbeing (Table 5.1).

Unfortunately, Keyes' (2002) research also showed that only a small proportion of the adult American population, one-fifth, is flourishing. It is not possible to say whether these findings would be replicated in other countries and cultures. However, given that mental disorders remain among the top 10 leading causes of disease burden worldwide, with no evidence of global reduction since 1990, it is reasonable to extrapolate that a significant part of the population is not flourishing.

Where clients position themselves in the mental health continuum and whether they are flourishing or languishing will have an impact on their

Table 5.1 Features of flourishing

	Psychological wellbeing	Social wellbeing
High positive affect	Self-acceptance	Social acceptance
High perceived quality of life	Personal growth	Actualisation
Low negative affect	Purpose in life	Contribution
	Environmental mastery	Coherence
	Autonomy	Integration
	Positive relations with others	

readiness for coaching and consequently on what they are able to achieve through the coaching programme. Coaches should add mental health to the list of considerations when contracting with clients and sponsors, assessing the needs of the clients/organisation and designing coaching programmes.

And, while recognising the limitations and professional boundaries, it is undeniable that coaches can play a key role in supporting clients to improve their mental wellbeing, which, in turn, will have a positive effect on their lives.

Some of the contributing factors to flourishing wellbeing, as described above, can be seen as integral to coaching, for example, helping clients to do the following:

- Find their sense of purpose and personal meaning
- Reconnect with themselves and their environment
- Reflect on their identity and values
- Adopt a healthy lifestyle
- Nurture positive emotions
- Pursue their goals.

On the other hand, coaching may provide the support a client needs to be able to consider their mental health issues and seek further help.

Rising to the challenge

As coaches, we are extremely privileged to be allowed into our clients' world and be a transient, supportive companion in their journeys. To serve all our clients well, it is crucial that we educate ourselves in mental health issues. The coaching industry, specifically training organisations, need to rise to the challenge and consider how training in this area can be improved to include recognition and management of mental health and psychological problems.

As professionals, we would do well to reflect on our biases and perceptions of mental illness and mental health and the impact they have on our practice and clients. Along with the privilege of being a coach comes the responsibility of meeting our clients where they are. We should acknowledge and validate their experiences, however uncomfortable and difficult these might be for them and us, and be able to give them our best professional support and guidance.

Clients' wellbeing

In a world where the aspiration is to have it all, how do we make space for our clients to express the full range of human experience and emotions including despair, sadness, failure and pessimism? How do we ensure that clients feel equally comfortable talking about mental health as they are discussing their physical ailments?

Awareness about mental health issues is not about diagnosing or labelling people. It is about nurturing compassion, flexibility and understanding about the human condition. Stopping mental illness stigma demands courage to embrace, understand, and discuss these issues in a transparent and helpful way. As Time to Change (a UK campaign to stop stigma around mental illness) puts it: 'Someone you know has a mental health problem. They just don't know how to tell you.' Let's make it easier for our clients to do so.

Personal accountability versus systemic pressures

Wellbeing goes beyond what is within the gift of individuals to change. And while individual choices can most certainly have an impact on that person's wellbeing, there could be detrimental factors which are outside their sphere of control. This is incredibly relevant as it helps the client understand where they can make the most difference and where their individual efforts may not be sufficient for the changes they desire and need.

As coaches, we need to be mindful of and reflect upon these potential limitations. Putting the onus of wellbeing and change upon individuals when the wider context may well be a significant contributor to their diminished wellbeing can be frustrating for the individual concerned.

As professional coaches, we need to reflect on our role and whether, instead of supporting people to improve their wellbeing, we can become an active part of a system that works against someone's wellbeing, making coaching a harmful intervention.

It is important for practitioners and commissioners of coaching services to acknowledge that there are significant external and systemic factors that can either hinder or foster people's wellbeing, including socio-economic circumstances, the environment, and their employment status, to name just a few.

Coaching for wellbeing may be more closely linked to personal wellbeing and it can support positive outcomes in the other areas highlighted. Other items might be outside the individual's control, depending on their personal circumstances. Professionally, we can face some hard ethical challenges. Let us explore some examples.

If you work with people in community settings, your clients could come from a range of backgrounds. Some of them may be experiencing financial, housing, health and/or other challenges, or have multiple needs. While they may be able to make choices and take actions that support their wellbeing, there may be limitations. If we place the sole responsibility for wellbeing on individuals themselves, we may be ignoring some significant systemic factors. Each individual's circumstances will be unique and they are the only ones who can find the right balance between acknowledging their individual responsibilities while accepting the aspects of their situation that are outwith their control.

In organisations, there can also be systemic pressures that are detrimental to employees' wellbeing, such as a culture of overwork and other unhealthy workplace practices, driven either by internal or external forces, such as economic and socio-political factors. For example, healthcare professionals' excessive workload and exposure to multiple stress factors that can adversely impact their psychological and physical wellbeing, leading to burnout, depression, anxiety disorders, sleeping disorders, among other illnesses (Søvold et al., 2021). Some of these issues are systemic and cannot be solved by the individuals themselves.

Another example of a challenging working environment is the finance sector, renowned for its deeply ingrained brutal workplace practices which, in the past, have been justified by high levels of pay. A survey of a small group of first-year analysts at global investment bank Goldman Sachs revealed widespread dissatisfaction and an average working week of 95 hours. Analysts report sleeping only five hours a night and, unsurprisingly, a sharp decline in mental and physical health (Goldman Sachs & Co., 2021).

Unfortunately, these challenges are not unique to healthcare or finance, as many other sectors experience challenging work conditions.

Ethical dilemmas emerge for coaches when coaching is perceived to be a tool to support employees, but which ignores systemic issues. A typical example could be commissioning coaching for wellbeing with an emphasis on resilience, under a narrative that employees need to become more resilient to deal with day-to-day work challenges. Resilience is important and it can support someone's wellbeing, but there is only so much resilience one can muster when dealing with intractable workplace practices, such as the ones described above. By placing the responsibility on individuals to develop better coping strategies and find their own ways to improve their wellbeing, there is a risk that systemic issues are not properly acknowledged and addressed.

Case study: Ad-hoc wellbeing support during the pandemic

After more than a year of coping with COVID-19 and having to deal with lockdowns that impacted daily life, the organisation saw that colleagues were finding it challenging to disconnect from work and be present in their lives. The organisation already had a wellbeing initiative in place, and they wanted to extend the offer to include coaching to help staff manage their personal wellbeing. The ultimate goal was to support colleagues to be the best versions of themselves. Through Bailey & French, the organisation offered a 60-minute virtual coaching session at a time and date that suited each employee. Sessions could be booked any day of the week, between 7 a.m. and 10 p.m., to provide flexibility around other commitments. Clients were also provided with a personal Wellbeing Action Plan template to complete, followed by a half-day of leave to bring the action plan to life. Feedback from clients was positive, with people using the opportunity to take a pause and reflect on what was important to them. Offering this type of support, when it mattered most, meant staff felt valued.

Evaluation

Evaluation is a core element of any professional coaching programme. While there are resources available elsewhere for coaches who would like to delve into this topic, in this section I will briefly explain some of the key considerations when designing, delivering and evaluating a coaching for wellbeing programme. The simplicity or indeed complexity of the evaluation methods you need will largely depend on the client commissioning the programme and their needs. Clarity on the outcomes expected from the programme is a great starting point; from there you will be able choose the best tools for the job.

Working with organisations

As explained elsewhere, organisations may deploy coaching as part of their wellbeing strategy. Among the outcomes they may be looking to evaluate are:

- Level of interest in the programme: number of people signing up for coaching.
- Individuals' engagement with the programme: attendance levels, completion (if programme has a set number of sessions) and personal feedback.
- Impact on individuals' levels of wellbeing: this can be measured using a recognised scale or questionnaire before and after the coaching intervention; follow-up after three or six months will be able to establish if changes were sustained over time. You can also compare levels of wellbeing between those participating in coaching and those who are not participating.
- Impact on staff retention: this can be evaluated by correlating staff's reported intention to leave the organisation and their levels of wellbeing, or it can be part of a more sophisticated methodology used to establish workforce trends across a span of time.
- Individual's satisfaction with the programme: qualitative questionnaires and self-reported measures.

As an example, the Institute for Employment Studies (IES) (Carter & Mason, 2021) conducted an evaluation of the Looking After You Too virtual coaching offer delivered to frontline primary care workers during the pandemic. During the first 14 months, 3,860 primary care staff received coaching. The coaching was commissioned by NHS England and NHS Improvement. The IES produced an infographic of the key findings, including:

- Significant improvement in wellbeing and resilience among staff who received coaching. Those who didn't showed deterioration of wellbeing and resilience levels.
- Those who received multiple coaching sessions had greater improvement in wellbeing in comparison to those who only had one session.
- Wellbeing scores declined between post-coaching and follow-up, but scores at follow-up remained higher than they were prior to coaching.

When working with community-based organisations, the same principles apply. In addition, these organisations may work with funders who have specific requirements regarding evaluation. They may favour a particular evaluation instrument and/or have strict guidelines for evaluation.

The best thing will be the impact assessment evaluation – its objective is to understand how effective the project was at achieving its aims. Here are some relevant questions that will need to be addressed:

- Did the coaching for wellbeing intervention lead to better outcomes? (you can use both quantitative as well as qualitative evidence)
- Was there a change? How big was the change?
- Was the change in line with expectations? Was there variation across demographic/geography, for example?

Using scales

Coaches can use many different scales to measure wellbeing levels. For my research project and the work I do in communities, I use the Warwick-Edinburgh Mental Wellbeing Scale (WEMWBS), which covers positive affect and psychological functioning (autonomy, competence, self-acceptance, personal growth) and interpersonal relationships. The WEMWBS has 14 positively phrased items, rated on a five-point Likert scale, which covers both hedonic and eudaimonic aspects of wellbeing and it is designed to assess the most relevant dimensions of mental wellbeing in the general population.

The WEMWBS was developed in the UK and has shown good validity, test/retest reliability (0.83), and internal consistency (0.91). This scale is widely used, and it has been developed to enable the monitoring of mental wellbeing in the general population and the evaluation of projects, programmes and policies. It is a tool recognised by both academics and policy-makers in the UK.

Below is a short list of other useful scales. Some are available free of charge for non-commercial use. It is likely that you need to get permission and/or pay a fee to use them in commercial programmes:

- Scales of Psychological Well-Being
- Mental Health Continuum Short Form
- Flourishing Scale
- Flourishing Index
- PERMA-Profiler
- Satisfaction with Life Scale
- Subjective Happiness Scale.

Part **3**

The BeWell Coaching for Wellbeing model

6 The BeWell Coaching for Wellbeing model

The BeWell model was developed during my doctoral studies. It is based on robust theoretical underpinnings and existing empirical evidence. I wanted a model that was flexible enough to be used across different demographics and settings, and based on both eudemonic and hedonic paradigms. Research points to both paradigms being useful to support an individual's wellbeing, and my professional experience of coaching in this area showed me that a holistic approach to wellbeing was helpful to clients, as it gave them flexibility to foster their wellbeing across different aspects of their lives – even if they experience challenges and limitations in some aspects. Therefore, and based on existing research, I decided to use psychological wellbeing theory as the main foundation for the model, combined with positive psychology cognitive behavioural principles.

This model has also been influenced by my personal philosophy of coaching, which is shaped by existential ideas (De Beauvoir, 2010; Sartre, 1992/1943; Yalom, 2020), specifically the beliefs that individuals have freedom to choose, they are responsible for their own actions, and that meaning and purpose are construed through learning and life experience. In simple terms, existential philosophers recognised that human beings have some degree of freedom to make choices and that choosing is not necessarily liberating. Sartre's view was that 'we are condemned to choose' and that 'the difference between choosing that which is there for me' as opposed to deceiving myself that any imaginable choice option is available is both significant and profound at every level of our experience' (Spinelli & Horner, 2008, p. 121). Furthermore, as human beings live in groups (society), conflicts can arise between the desires of the 'self' and societal accepted norms. This can cause 'angst' (Sartre, 1992/1943), and internal turmoil surrounding the choices one makes in life.

Coaching through the existential lens can be useful for clients in terms of raising self-awareness and the acceptance of conflicts, imbalances, and challenges clients encounter when making choices and living an authentic life. The existential approach allows clients to align and understand their values in relation to their world-view and their active (existence) role in it. It also encourages them to take responsibility in the existential sense of the word: 'Responsibility. Consciousness [of] being the incontestable author of an event or object' (Sartre, 1992/1943, p. 707). Considering these thoughts, my approach is one that encourages clients to take responsibility for their choices, assess their lives realistically and explore how they can derive meaning from it.

A note on cognitive behavioural principles

Cognitive theory, as pioneered by Albert Ellis (1962), describes the relationship between thinking and behaviour. Cognitive theory posits that (A) an event, (B) behaviour and (C) the consequence are interlinked, with people experiencing either healthy or dysfunctional cognition about events, which leads to functional or dysfunctional consequences, respectively.

Beck and Beck (1995) combined behavioural theory with cognitive theory, creating the basis for Cognitive Behavioural Therapy (CBT) which is organised around the concepts of automatic thoughts and schemas. This can be framed as Figure 6.1.

> Automatic thoughts are surface level cognitions and are the actual words or images that pass through a person's mind. Assumptions are intermediate level beliefs and consist of attitudes, rules and assumptions. Core beliefs are the deepest level of beliefs and these beliefs are rigid, global and overgeneralised. Cognitive therapy aims to evaluate and modify unhelpful thinking and behaviour (Beck, 1995).
>
> (Palmer & Gyllensten, 2008, p. 39)

CBT is supported by a robust evidence base (Butler et al., 2006; Hofmann et al., 2012) and is commonly used to treat a wide range of disorders, including depression and anxiety (Kerns et al., 2016).

> According to cognitive behavioural theory, the social and interpersonal experiences have a strong impact on clients' perception of themselves (self-schemas), others (schemas about others) and the world (schemas about the world) and have a strong impact on the character of their experiences, their human features, and their anticipation of the future.
>
> (Prasko et al., 2012, p. 5)

Figure 6.1 The CBT triangle: the relationship between thoughts, emotions and behaviours

What we think affects
how we act and feel

Thought

Emotion

Behaviour

What we feel affects
how we think and do

What we do affects
how we think and feel

Third-wave CBT

Although founded in the cognitive-behavioural traditions, CBT has evolved to embrace other theoretical bases in the so-called third-wave CBT, including working with mindfulness, compassion, acceptance, and values. These are aligned to coaching, in particular, coaching for wellbeing that is based on the eudaimonic paradigm.

Third-wave CBT has the following features:

- Includes client's relationship to emotions and thoughts
- Emphasises emotions, mindfulness, relationships, values and goals
- Values philosophically-based interventions
- Includes compassion-focused therapy, acceptance and commitment therapy, dialectical behavioural therapy.

In coaching, cognitive behavioural techniques and approaches, including third-wave ideas, are often used in a non-therapeutic way to support clients in raising awareness of their unhelpful thinking patterns and in adopting more rational and helpful explanatory styles (Palmer & Gyllensten, 2008). CBT principles are also used to challenge unhelpful beliefs, and they can support those who want to establish new thought patterns and behaviours. Palmer and Gyllensten explain that when clients' reactions to events and experiences in their lives are based on unhelpful thinking patterns, cognitive-behavioural coaching (CBC) approaches can support clients in developing emotional agility as outlined by Smith (2017, p. 353):

> The cognitive approach advises the coach to work with the client to 'dispute' and question the validity of these attitudes and beliefs. The objective is to help the client out of their habitual 'pessimistic automatic thoughts' to consider alternatives and thus choose an interpretation that generates a more helpful consequence, referred to as 'performance enhancing thoughts'.

This approach helps clients achieve a more balanced and objective view of their experience. It also enhances their ability to flex their thinking and look at events in their lives from a range of perspectives.

As part of my research, specifically when considering the theories for the coaching model, I decided to explore CBT principles, to raise awareness among clients about the relationship between thoughts, feelings and behaviours, and help them identify unhelpful thinking patterns that could be having a detrimental impact on their ability to pursue their wellbeing goals. For example, clients who tend to see the world using an 'all-or-nothing lens' tend to find it challenging to build new habits in an incremental way; they are also more likely to 'throw the baby out with the bath water' when things go wrong. 'All or nothing' is one of many unhelpful thinking patterns or cognitive distortions; these tend to be inaccurate, and often negatively biased.

Case study: Zoe's thinking patterns

Zoe was working on building a healthier lifestyle, particularly focused on regular physical exercise, eating well and meditating on a regular basis. But she would stop all these things if one activity did not go according to plan. So let's say that she managed to follow her plan from Monday to Wednesday, and then on Wednesday she arrived late from work and missed her workout. Instead of continuing with her plans, she would stop all her efforts until the following week. In her mind, that week was 'a write-off' and she needed to wait until the following Monday to 'start over'. That is not a helpful way of thinking as:

1 It ignores the good work that has gone into the week until that point.
2 It makes her feel defeated in her efforts.
3 Between Wednesday and the following Monday, she can engage in behaviour that is not getting her close to her goal and which could, in fact, have the opposite effect.

She would then experience lower levels of self-efficacy and potentially negative emotions about herself and her goals. When exploring this pattern of thinking and behaviour, Zoe quickly realised that it was unhelpful, but it had been her 'autopilot' across different areas of her life. By gaining an insight into her automatic thoughts, with the help of the coach, Zoe was able to stop herself before getting into autopilot mode. It was not always easy, but slowly she managed to temper her 'all-or-nothing' tendencies. This had a positive impact on how she progressed towards her wellbeing goals and other areas of her life.

Here are some other examples of how these unhelpful thinking patterns can adversely impact a client's wellbeing efforts:

- *Discounting the positive*: Clients who discount the positive may have a harder time identifying and connecting with the good things that happen in their daily lives to create little moments of joy and increase their experience of positive emotions.
- *Should statements*: If a client's thoughts revolve around 'should', 'ought to' and 'must have', they may feel guilty and place the blame on themselves for having a negative experience.
- *Catastrophising*: This is when clients go straight to the worst-case scenario in any given situation. This can increase their negative feelings and limit their ability to see opportunities.
- *Overgeneralisation*: People who overgeneralise often use statements including words such as 'always', 'never', 'every' or 'all'. Clients may see themselves

as 'never able to do a particular thing', or use expressions, such as 'people like me do not achieve these types of goals' or 'do not do a particular type of activity'.

I have included a list of cognitive distortions in the Appendix, the coach's toolkit, alongside some exercises for you to help your client manage them more effectively.

BeWell Coaching for Wellbeing

The model has three pillars – Be, Relate and Act – delivered over four coaching phases (Figure 6.2). Given the fluid nature of coaching, this is a framework that can be flexed and adapted according to the needs and interests of the clients. It embodies the multifaceted and complex nature of wellbeing delivered within the spirit of coaching, which is a dynamic process, driven by the clients' agenda. The model was originally designed to be delivered in group settings, which is the focus of Chapter 7.

Figure 6.2 The BeWell Coaching for Wellbeing model

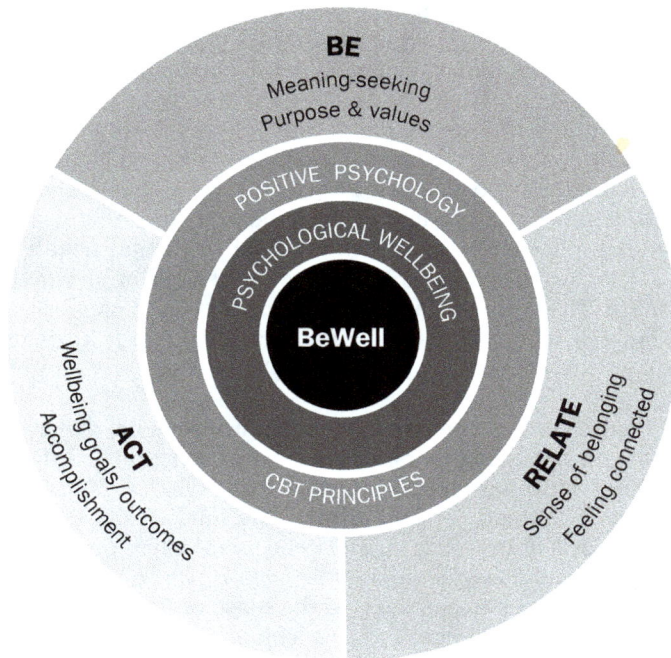

Source: Nacif (2021).

The three pillars of *BeWell*

1 Be: meaning seeking; purpose and values

This first pillar of the programme supports clients to achieve clarity around their values, purpose and the meaning they want to bring to their lives. This work is supported by two components: 'meaning-seeking' and 'purpose and values'. It is an opportunity for clients to work on their wellbeing vision. This pillar aligns to the purpose in life, personal growth, autonomy and self-acceptance of Ryff's psychological wellbeing theory (Ryff, 1989).

Research has demonstrated the positive impact of meaning in one's life and wellbeing. Increased meaning has been associated with higher life satisfaction (Steger, 2018), self-esteem (Ryff, 1989), lower rates of anxiety and depression (Steger et al., 2006) and better physical health (Steger et al., 2009). Meaning is a crucial part of the eudaimonic concept of wellbeing. In this model, I leaned towards the existential approach to meaning, specifically Frankl's idea of will-to-meaning, which is about our ability to seek meaning in our daily experiences, even in tough circumstances.

The concept of will-to-meaning is helpful if we want to make coaching for wellbeing inclusive to the widest number of people as possible. Wellbeing and health have not been immune to the proliferation of the 'Insta life' and other forms of social media, where people display a perfect and curated portrait of their experiences. If you Google 'wellbeing', you will get millions of hits. Inevitably, some of the pages displayed will have images of stones, nature, yoga poses and the like. These landscapes tend to evoke feelings of beauty, calm, and relaxation. But, as we know, wellbeing is deeply personal and, if we want to make coaching for wellbeing accessible to a wide range of people, then we need to work with the limitations and challenges many are facing. These could include working in a demanding role and organisation, living with a terminal illness or a long-term physical or mental health condition, having to battle through social or economic challenges, or just having a 'normal' messy life. The will-to-meaning concept helps us to support our clients under the most difficult and challenging circumstances. It helps us become inclusive in our thinking, instead of creating rigid parameters for our clients' wellbeing.

The same principles can be applied to the purpose in life dimension, which draws heavily on existential perspectives and is concerned with supporting people to create meaning and direction in their lives (Ryff & Singer, 2008, p. 22). Purpose in life and personal growth are intrinsically linked and they are used in the BeWell model to support clients in delving into how actively engaged they are with these themes in their lives. By doing this, clients are able to increase their own self-acceptance, in the sense of a 'self-evaluation that is long-term and involves awareness, and acceptance of, both personal strengths and weaknesses' (Ryff & Singer, 2008, p. 21). By exploring their purpose and values, clients also develop a stronger sense of self, their wellbeing needs and aspirations. This, in turn, gives clients clarity about who they are and what they want to achieve in their lives, increasing their autonomy, i.e. how they perceive to be in control of their own behaviour and goals (Ryan, 2017), which can lead to improved levels of wellbeing.

Key points

- Meaning and purpose as important aspects of a wellbeing vision.
- Positive impact of meaning on physical and mental health and wellbeing.
- Wellbeing can be enhanced despite difficult circumstances, if we use a will-to-meaning lens.

2 Relate: sense of belonging; feeling connected

The second pillar (Relate) includes 'sense of belonging' and 'feeling connected'. Both are concerned with psychological theory's dimension of positive relationships. It highlights the 'interpersonal realm as a central feature of a positive, well-lived life' (Ryff & Singer, 2008, p. 21). This pillar is also aligned with Seligman's 'R' (positive relationships) in his PERMA theory, which considers social connections as a key component for people's wellbeing, and one of the most important aspects of our lives (Seligman, 2012). Social contact is a fundamental human need and relatedness is essential for wellbeing (Argyle & Crossland, 1987; Baumeister & Leary, 1995; Deci & Ryan, 1991).

This part of the model invites clients to explore the different aspects of their lives that give them a sense of belonging and connecting with others. Usually, this dimension is embedded in clients' vision of wellbeing, which they developed early in the coaching process and as part of the first pillar. Over many years working with wellbeing, I am yet to encounter a client who does not include in their vision some sort of connection or relationship with other people and/or groups of people. The possibilities in this area of life are limitless, from romantic relationships, family and friends to connections with communities of interest, work, creative and artistic endeavours, sports, leisure, volunteering, or activism, to name just a few. Depending on the clients' interests, there could be an overlap between connection, belonging and engagement, both in the sense of flow and fully immersing oneself in an activity, and in getting involved in something bigger than oneself.

Key points

- Belonging and connections are crucial cornerstones of wellbeing.
- Clients can explore this area from myriad perspectives, across all areas of their lives.
- Social connection is a fundamental human need.

3 Act: wellbeing goals and outcomes: accomplishments

From trivial pursuits to obsessions of a lifetime

In Chapter 3, I wrote about goals in wellbeing coaching, where I shared my fondness for Little's personal projects (1989), which give clients flexibility in how to pursue whatever they need to improve their sense of wellbeing. Whereas for some people, having SMART goals is helpful, other approaches to goals are also effective. Depending on the client group you are working with, they may have unique needs and adopting a flexible approach to wellbeing goals and outcomes is important. In addition, because wellbeing is a multi-faceted concept that touches every single aspect of the client's life, you may be surprised by what emerges from the coaching process regarding the things clients want to change in their lives to enhance their wellbeing.

Clients have unique needs in terms of their wellbeing goals and outcomes, which are, of course, an important part of the coaching process. These will naturally emerge from their wellbeing vision. In practice, there is a possibility that the initial goals presented by the client may change during the course of the coaching programme, as they explore the different aspects of their wellbeing, some of which they may not have had an opportunity to reflect on previously. For clients who have a clear goal, or goals, they want to pursue, this pillar provides practical coaching support, such as action planning and accountability, to keep them on track. For those who are still considering their goals, this pillar gives them plenty of opportunities to explore.

Self-efficacy and accomplishment

This pillar can be useful to support self-efficacy and motivation. This can be done through 'baby steps' towards a wellbeing outcome or behaviour; by encouraging little moments of joy and positive emotions; and by exposing clients to a range of coaching and positive psychology interventions for them to try and test.

Clients can try out wellbeing activities such as writing journal entries, doing mindfulness exercises, spending more time in the garden, connecting with friends, cooking more and doing something fun.

Apart from potential positive wellbeing outcomes that could emerge from these activities, the objective here is also to increase the client's sense of accomplishment, which can encourage them to continue or take up an activity, and perhaps set more ambitious goals. This sense of accomplishment gives clients a positive emotional experience, which can affect their wellbeing. This third pillar can also be associated with the environmental mastery dimension in Ryff's (1989) psychological wellbeing model, as it can support individuals' ability to choose or change their surrounding context using physical or mental actions as well as being able to control events.

Key points

- A flexible approach to wellbeing goals is key to supporting individual needs.
- Wellbeing goals can emerge from all spheres of life.

• 'Baby steps' and/or coaching and positive psychology interventions can be used to build the client's self-efficacy, motivation and a sense of accomplishment.

The BeWell delivery framework

You can use your existing coaching approach and techniques to guide your clients through the three pillars of the model – Be, Relate and Act – based on the theoretical knowledge and understanding shared throughout this book. For those who would like to have a starting point, I will walk you through the practical steps you can take to deliver a BeWell Coaching for Wellbeing programme. This is only a suggested framework. There are hundreds of useful coaching tools available for this work and I am highlighting only a small sample of them. It is also important to remember that tools are not always necessary or needed, and coaches should harness their coaching skills and approach to meet clients' needs and preferences.

As mentioned above, the BeWell model has three pillars – Be, Relate and Act – delivered over four coaching phases, which do not need to be delivered in a linear way. Below is a snapshot of the delivery framework, followed by a more detailed explanation of each phase.

Coaches often ask me how many sessions are needed to deliver the programme. The length of the programme will depend on the individual needs of the client, the resources available for the delivery of the coaching programme, and whether the programme is part of a wider wellbeing project or not. A programme of four to six sessions is a good starting point and, if possible, flexibility to extend by a further four to six sessions if necessary. The frequency of the sessions will depend on the client group, fortnightly and monthly being my preferred options. Spacing sessions out gives clients time in between sessions to consider the learning and changes they are making. Using these parameters will mean that the programme will last a few months, a good chunk of time for clients to start to implement sustainable change. Table 6.1 presents a possible framework for the BeWell model.

Phase 1

At the start of the coaching programme, the focus is on exploring:

1 What wellbeing means to the client: the coach helps the client to understand their experience of wellbeing and the factors they believe contribute to and/or hinder their wellbeing. If a tool is needed, the Wheel of Wellbeing can be helpful at this stage.
2 Wellbeing vision: the butterfly exercise, described below, can help the client develop their vision. This helps them explore their hopes, dreams and aspirations. You can also use some of the strategies listed in Chapter 3.

Table 6.1 Framework for the BeWell model

Pillars	Be, Relate, Act			
	Phase 1	**Phase 2**	**Phase 3**	**Phase 4**
Suggested coaching tools	Wellbeing vision You: the butterfly Wheel of wellbeing	Future self Meaning Identifying personal values Peak experience Life story Self-acceptance, self-compassion and kindness exercise	Strengths Your best self Hope exercises Gratitude letter	Celebrating success Future-proof wellbeing and planning
Further tools and positive psychology interventions	Challenging perceptions and thoughts Wellbeing plan PPIs: savouring gratitude hope, compassion and kindness	Challenging perceptions and thoughts Wellbeing plan PPIs: savouring gratitude hope, compassion and kindness	Challenging perceptions and thoughts Wellbeing plan PPIs: savouring gratitude hope, compassion and kindness	Challenging perceptions and thoughts Wellbeing plan PPIs: savouring gratitude hope, compassion and kindness

This initial part of the programme is designed to support clients to explore what wellbeing means to them, including all the elements they perceive as contributing to their own personal wellbeing. As part of this discussion, clients are introduced to the ideas of 'identity, change and transformation' through a butterfly analogy. This is a fun and tangible way to guide their journey during the coaching programme, while serving as an emblem of their 'wellbeing transformation'. I sometimes use butterfly images, stickers, cards or garden ornaments to give to clients so they have something tangible to represent their journey. I chose to use butterflies because of their symbolic representation of endurance, change and life. People tend to be familiar with the butterfly's metamorphosis and can use this metaphor when considering the transformations they want in their own lives and wellbeing.

The butterfly exercise

Each step of the butterfly exercise (Figure 6.3) is designed to support reflection and self-awareness:

- What are your colours? – Clients explore their sense of self, who they are, their feelings, using colours.
- Are you ready to fly? – Clients consider whether they feel ready to make changes.

Figure 6.3 The butterfly exercise: symbol of transformation

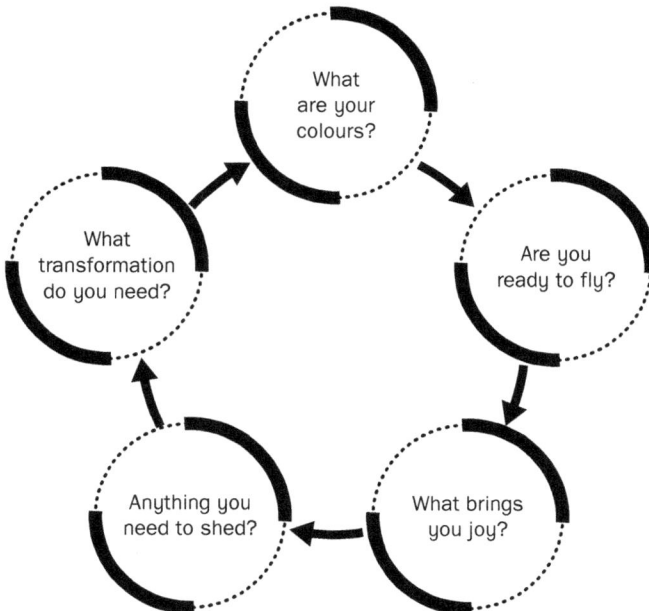

Source: Nacif (2021).

- What brings you joy? – This is an invitation for clients to expand their understanding of everything in their lives that brings them joy and to consider the presence or absence of these things at this time in their lives.
- Anything you need to shed? – Clients explore what 'needs to go' to support the development of their wellbeing, for example, negative habits, thought patterns and attitudes.
- What transformation do you need? – This is a chance for clients to consider their vision for wellbeing.

Phase 2

Following on from the deep dive into personal meanings of wellbeing, their wellbeing vision and the exploration of self and transformation, clients can move on to work on their life experiences in relation to meaning-seeking, the role of personal values and life purpose, and how these impact their sense of wellbeing. Meaning is linked to both psychological wellbeing theory and positive psychology. One of the coaching exercises I like using in this phase is the future self-exercise, from the Co-active Coaching approach (Kimsey-House et al., 2010, p. 235). This is a visualisation exercise that invites the client to meet their 'higher self', a self who is powerful, fulfilled and who can become a reference for the client's vision of themselves. There are limitations to visualisation exercises. Not every client enjoys them and there are those who have aphantasia, which means they are not able to create mental images with their mind's eye.

This phase is also suitable for exploring the client's values and their purpose. Some of the options to work with your clients on values include:

1 The values exercise, where you ask your client to consider a long list of values and rank their top five.
2 Values cards.
3 Peak experience: ask the client to think of a time when they felt on top of the world, and/or experiences they felt were just perfect; explore the scenario as thoroughly as possible and then try to identify which values are associated with that experience.

You can also help clients explore their sense of purpose. Useful exercises for that include:

1 How do you want to be remembered? Ask the client to write their own obituary. Morbid as it seems, this helps clients focus on the core of what they would like their lives to entail.
2 If you had only 12 months to live, how would you choose to live your life? The same principles apply in this exercise, with the spotlight on a very short period of time, considering the span of a lifetime.

3   Life story: Ask clients to explore the 'stories' in their lives and evaluate these narratives in the light of their sense of purpose and values. Ask them to write the 'old story' (where they have been), the 'present story' (where they are) and the 'new story' (where they would like to be), ask them to explore change and the strengths they can draw on to attain their desired wellbeing outcomes.

Purpose and meaning tend to be intertwined as we derive meaning from a life of purpose and when our lives are aligned with our values. As explained earlier, when developing this model, I favoured Frankl's 'will-to-meaning' concept, which means we are able to find meaning and purpose in our lives, even in challenging circumstances. Everyday meaning and purpose are something to be cherished and encouraged. This quote, from King, Heintzelman and Ward (2016), sums up the spirit of everyday meaning: 'Rather than being mysterious and inaccessible, meaning in life is rooted in quotidian circumstances and is a surprisingly common human experience' (p. 212). Interestingly, in his book *Flow* (1990), Csikszentmihalyi talks about individuals who have autotelic personalities. By that he means people who can engage in meaningful ways with whatever tasks they need to complete in their daily lives; the purpose is found within the individual and is dependent on the task.
    Here are some meaning exercises you can use with your clients:

1   Ask clients to take pictures of their everyday experiences which are meaningful. They can create an inspiring collage or a 'meaning board'. They can use other ways to capture meaningful moments, things, people, experiences, such as writing, art, music, or any other methods they enjoy.
2   Your best self exercise.
3   Meaning-making writing exercise: ask clients to reflect about positive outcomes that have come out of negative events.

The likelihood is that during the work done in phases 1 and 2, it has become apparent which relationships are important for the client, and/or from where they get their sense of belonging. If this factor seems to be missing and, depending on the client's circumstances, you may choose to bring it to the fore for exploration and discussion.

Phase 3

This phase emphasises clients' choices, encouraging them to raise self-awareness and understand the strategies that will work for them to sustain change and boost motivation levels. There may be a recalibration of the vision and wellbeing outcomes. Because wellbeing is not something that the client will have 'done and dusted' by the end of the coaching programme, this phase is important to maximise their chances of creating sustainable change. Raising self-awareness about external and internal barriers, such as mindset, fluctuating motivation levels and unhelpful thinking patterns and beliefs, as well as helping them develop strategies to manage these, will equip them to continue their wellbeing journey. A useful topic to use in your coaching in this phase is 'hope'. When the going gets tough, hope can keep us going.

> According to hope theory, hope reflects individuals' perceptions of their capacities to (a) clearly conceptualise goals; (b) develop the specific strategies to reach those goals (pathways thinking); and (c) initiate and sustain the motivation for using those strategies (agency thinking)'.
>
> (Joseph, 2015, p. 483)

Among the exercises you can use to help clients increase hope are:

- Sharing and recalling past successes
- Mind-mapping the different paths they can use to achieve their goals, including how they can deal with obstacles
- Connecting to their vision and their compelling reasons
- Visualising achieving their wellbeing goals.

Phase 4

This phase is about consolidating the work done so far and, of course, celebrating the client's successes and their commitment to their wellbeing vision. Unlike other types of coaching where the end of the coaching programme can signal the client achieving their goal, when it comes to wellbeing, it is about committing for the long run. One of the most valuable outcomes of the coaching is the client's increased self-awareness and understanding of personal wellbeing needs and aspirations. Their learning will enable them to continue their wellbeing journey, assured that they have the knowledge to deal with the inevitable ups and down, and recognising the value and benefits of making the right choices for them.

As explained before, these phases do not need to be delivered in a linear way. The BeWell Coaching for Wellbeing model is meant to be flexible. It has all the ingredients to support clients to improve their wellbeing, without being prescriptive, which would go against the ethos of coaching and the philosophy that influenced the development of this model.

7 The BeWell Group Coaching for Wellbeing model

My original research in coaching for wellbeing was designed for groups. Given that relatedness and belonging are crucial to our wellbeing, I was curious to find out if groups could add a collective dimension to the process of coaching for wellbeing.

The findings of the research confirmed that, as a collective entity, the group was the catalyst for change and an active factor in client's perception of their wellbeing. It enabled the clients to experience positive relationships and relatedness, compounded by a sense of belonging and connection. The group environment was also conducive to fostering new perspectives, as it became a sounding board for new ideas, thinking and reflection, helping clients develop their vision for wellbeing. Also significant was the collective accountability among group members, which propelled clients into action, implementing change, celebrating achievements and developing self-efficacy.

Although research into group coaching is still emerging, existing evidence points to the advantages group coaching can offer individuals, communities and organisations. In this chapter, we will explore some of this evidence and the practicalities of delivering group coaching for wellbeing in different contexts.

What is group coaching?

There is often confusion about the definition of group coaching and team coaching, with these terms being used interchangeably. They are distinct in purpose and nature. In group coaching, clients come together to work on a particular theme, but each individual has their own personal goals. These individuals do not know each other and the coach joins the group from its very beginning, experiencing the growth of the group and its dynamics as the coaching process progresses. Team coaching, on the other hand, requires team members to work together towards a collective goal for the whole team, which is usually aligned with organisational aims and objectives. The coach joins an existing team, with pre-existing dynamics.

I have defined group coaching as 'a collaborative and time-limited small-group process in which a professionally-trained coach uses coaching tools and principles to work with a group of individuals on their own personal goals and/ or outcomes' (Nacif, 2021).

Why use group coaching for wellbeing?

Virtually all wellbeing theories highlight the importance of relating and belonging to our wellbeing. Interacting with other people, sharing and feeling connected can have a positive impact on us. Therefore, if the objective of the coaching is to support people to flourish, working in groups can be a natural fit. In saying that, group work is not for everyone, nor is it meant to replace individual coaching, but it can be an effective solution, alongside other wellbeing initiatives. And, for individuals who are looking for a group of like-minded individuals, or for a group of people who share the same life experiences, groups can be effective.

Group coaching for wellbeing in organisations

Group coaching can support organisations, helping deliver on their wellbeing strategy by bringing people from across teams, functions and geographies together to work on specific wellbeing topics or simply to support their personal wellbeing. The advantages of group coaching for wellbeing in organisations are many. From a pragmatic perspective, group coaching is scalable and more cost-effective in comparison to individual coaching. It follows that group coaching can therefore be made available to a wider number of employees, across the whole organisation. The collective nature of it tends to encourage connections that go beyond the duration of the programme while fostering the value of collaboration and collective contribution.

As highlighted in Chapter 1, some of the wellbeing challenges facing organisations go beyond the role of individual responsibility. By bringing people together, group coaching can encourage conversations that can ultimately support changes in culture and working practices. It can help organisations to navigate the balance between individual's accountability and systemic changes. The ripple impact of individuals going back to their teams and sharing their learning, combined with a deeper understanding of shared narratives which reflect the experiences of individuals across the organisation, may spark the enthusiasm for collective solutions and innovative practices.

As an example, a medium-sized organisation in the UK commissioned group coaching for wellbeing during the COVID-19 pandemic to support members of staff who were flagging, due to resulting pressures. They were looking for a cost-effective solution that would support employees to increase their levels of personal wellbeing in this challenging time. During the first year of the programme, and as a direct result of the cross-fertilisation of ideas brought about by staff experiencing group coaching, they started to develop a wellbeing champion's programme and genuinely engaged with employees across the organisation, aiming to enhance their wellbeing strategy and improve workplace practices to further support staff's wellbeing.

Ideally, coaching for wellbeing would be aligned with and be part of a well-designed wellbeing strategy. Organisations wanting to address the needs of specific demographics within their business would do well to put some thought into leveraging the benefits of this coaching modality. The supportive and encouraging environment of groups can be helpful for employees returning to work after a period of absence due to illness; staff living with long-term physical and mental health conditions; or new parents getting back to work after parental leave.

Depending on the needs of the organisation and its employees, a thematic approach to group coaching for wellbeing may be helpful, such as running groups on general wellbeing, understanding and managing stress, coping with feeling overwhelmed, plus belonging and inclusion for improved wellbeing, among others. As mentioned before, it is important to recognise the balance between individual responsibility and systemic pressures.

A study (Gyllensten & Palmer, 2005) into group coaching involving 31 participants of a UK finance organisation found that levels of anxiety and stress went down for those participating in the group-coaching programme compared to a control group. Participants reported the coaching to be highly effective.

Other areas of research, such as group coaching for leadership development, point to clients experiencing increased self-awareness, self-confidence, shared support and improved understanding of relationships with others (Bonneywell, 2016; Mbokota & Reid, 2022).

These benefits are intrinsic to the nature of group work itself and it is reasonable to extrapolate that group coaching for wellbeing will impact clients in similar ways. Research findings specific to group coaching for wellbeing (Nacif, 2021) show that group coaching improves clients' wellbeing by promoting positive emotions and self-awareness, and by flexing clients' thinking by exposing them to multiple perspectives while interacting with other group members. Clients also report that collective accountability can be a powerful tool to encourage and inspire wellbeing goals and actions.

Group coaching for wellbeing in community settings

Considering societal needs and the recognition of the role wellbeing plays in all spheres of life, group coaching for wellbeing is well placed to support individuals in a variety of community contexts.

My research into coaching for wellbeing in the community showed that participants' wellbeing levels improved after completing the programme. Interestingly, some of the themes and benefits that emerged from the research are clearly helpful to clients in various aspects of their lives. For example, clients reported increased self-confidence and awareness of having more choices available to them to improve their wellbeing than they initially thought. As their self-confidence increased through the group work, so did their self-belief, enabling them to contemplate a more ambitious vision for their wellbeing, and for their lives. This is aligned with Bandura's (1997) theory of self-efficacy, which posits that people's beliefs in their ability to achieve something are related to their motivation to take the required action in the direction of their goals. These feelings were reinforced by collective accountability. As a result, they are more likely to take action and effect change. Clients supported, challenged each other and, ultimately, held themselves and each person in the group accountable for the work they had committed to doing together.

Another important topic raised by this research was the role of the group in increasing experiences of positive emotions and belonging among members. One of the groups I investigated for the research was a group of people living with HIV. The feedback showed that the impact of positive relationships within the group was particularly significant for group members who felt lonely and isolated. Research shows that HIV-positive people are more prone to loneliness and isolation due to HIV stigma, homophobia or transphobia, which often cause emotional distress (Erenrich et al., 2019; Fekete et al., 2018). Most people living with HIV experience some degree of stigma, which can be detrimental to their wellbeing (Earnshaw & Chaudoir, 2009). Clients in this group voiced that there was 'no stigma' in the group, which indicates that temporarily they were able to experience interactions without feeling judged, which seemed to be affirming for clients. They reported that the group aspect of the coaching programme was significant because 'people are lonely', again underlining the experience of this particular demographic. The signs of hope and optimism were in stark contrast to some of the individual narratives shared at the beginning of the programme, which reflected loneliness, isolation and sadness in some clients. This is not to say that these challenging feelings were fully alleviated by the end of the programme (which was not the intention), but clients did report an increase in positive feelings. Clients' reflections confirmed the power of shared experiences and narratives, which through group cohesion and collaboration supported the wellbeing of individuals.

Among other findings are a rich variety of wellbeing actions and outcomes which reflect the complexity of wellbeing as a construct, from reconnecting with estranged family members, going back to further education, creating a 'wellbeing routine', taking up a hobby and working less, to personal changes, such as trying to increase self-acceptance and self-compassion.

The group coaching process

For those who would like to explore group coaching as part of their wellbeing offer, this section explains very briefly the group coaching process, which is outside the scope of this book. Group coaching allows clients to bear witness to others' emotions, feelings and experiences, including achievements in their wellbeing, which can be reassuring, inspirational and propelling. In group coaching, the collection itself becomes the engine of the coaching process. For this engine to work as well as it can, there are three cogs: trust, collaboration and challenge (Figure 7.1). Trust allows clients to be open and honest with each other during the sessions. The second cog is collaboration. Clients work together to support individual members of the group as well as the group as a collective.

A fully functioning group provides a safety net for individuals, allowing them to take risks and be vulnerable when sharing their thoughts and feelings.

Figure 7.1 Creating a safe environment for groups

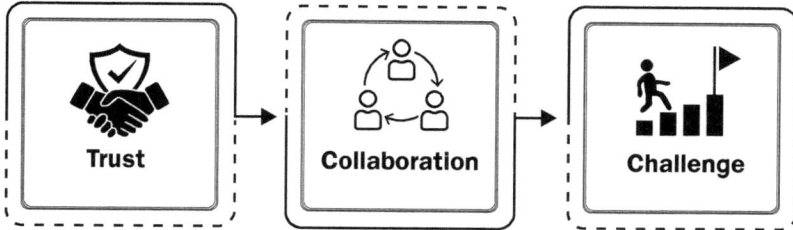

Support becomes collective, as opposed to individual, as is the case in one-to-one experiences. For example, the group may rally around someone who is facing a particular challenge and/or is finding it difficult to take action. Groups also tend to normalise experiences which may have been perceived by individuals as unique to them. The reaction: 'I'm glad you say that. I thought it was only me who felt that way!' is an example of this phenomenon. Yalom (1995) called this experience 'universality', when group members realise that they are not alone in their feelings, thoughts and problems. He also highlighted it as one of the factors that make group work effective.

With a sense of psychological safety, clients feel comfortable challenging each other, which promotes group cohesion, another crucial factor for the success of group work. The group process allows similarities and differences to emerge, raising self-awareness and contributing to widening clients' horizons in relation to their wellbeing. Unfortunately, not all groups will work without hiccups. Sometimes the difficulties experienced by the group can be part of the learning and growth of the individuals in it; occasionally you may encounter a group that does not work well. To minimise issues, contracting well at the beginning of the coaching programme is crucial.

7.1 Case study: community setting

A not-for-profit organisation, which supports women from disadvantaged communities, wanted to add coaching to their client offering. The primary aim was to foster women's sense of wellbeing to address health inequalities in the local area, with disadvantaged people experiencing the worst health outcomes. The coaching was delivered to groups of up to 10 women over six coaching sessions, lasting two hours each, delivered face-to-face, over a period of six weeks. I used the BeWell Group Coaching model. The evaluation included pre- and post-coaching wellbeing questionnaires (the Warwick-Edinburgh Mental Wellbeing Scale), which showed significant improvement in participants' wellbeing. A qualitative survey was also used. It included three points: What was your favourite part of the programme?; Was there anything you did not enjoy?; and Share one specific change that you will implement to improve your wellbeing.

Key considerations when working with community-led organisations:

- Coaching programmes may need to be aligned to the outcomes of the larger projects, so it is important to understand the aims of the programme and how it will be evaluated. Some organisations have specific scales, surveys and questionnaires they want to use for evaluation.
- It is important to understand the context of the client groups you will be working with; think about any changes or adaptions needed for the delivery of the programme, such as language and disability.
- Be mindful of systemic factors which may be contributing to people's lack of wellbeing, and the limitations clients may be facing in their lives.

Although the programme in the case study was commissioned under a project to tackle health inequalities, working with wellbeing in its wider sense was seen as instrumental to support these women in distinct aspects of their lives. In the first session, clients were surprised to realise how many factors influenced their wellbeing, with some voicing they had expected the group to be talking only about food and exercise. The wellbeing vision for each of the participants was unique and personal, prompting interesting discussions in the group. Several aspects of the model, delivered over a number of sessions, catered to people's individual needs while keeping the collective aspect of the group.

Case study: an organisation's wellbeing offering

A series of wellbeing coaching programmes were delivered to a medium-sized organisation. Coaching was part of the company's wellbeing offer to employees. A staff survey highlighted wellbeing concerns as a priority for employees, so the company decided to offer some extra support. The coaching programme was delivered online to groups of up to eight people, over four fortnightly coaching sessions, lasting 90 minutes each. The programme was open to members of staff in a particular grade. The promotion and recruitment for the programme were done internally by the organisation. I used the BeWell Group Coaching model, adapting it to include an added focus on 'work and wellbeing', for example, by explicitly adding a work dimension to the discussions around wellbeing vision, strengths and action planning. The organisation applied its own questionnaire to evaluate the programme.

The wellbeing challenges were similar among the clients, specifically related to workload and company policies and practices that were perceived to adversely affect employees. There were a mix of personal and work-focused outcomes for individuals in the groups, and a particular emphasis on actions for many participants. Some patterns emerging from the different groups included: reflecting on daily choices that supported their wellbeing; seeking out opportunities to use their strengths more frequently in the workplace; recognising opportunities to change and influence change in existing working practices, and focusing on rewarding work whenever possible.

Key considerations when delivering wellbeing coaching programmes in corporate settings:

- *Objectives*: What is the purpose of the programme and how does it fit in with the organisation's needs, aims and other services the organisation offers to support employees? What data is available, such as staff surveys and engagement levels? Be mindful of systemic issues affecting employees' wellbeing.
- *Recruitment*: Who will be participating in the programme and what are the plans for recruitment?
- *Logistics*: Who will be booking venues/catering and, if delivering online, whose platform will you be using? What are the implications for personal data handling and protection? How will you communicate with clients before the programme commencing and who will be the point of contact during the programme?
- *Boundaries and confidentiality*: This refers to the organisation's expectations regarding feedback from the programme and client confidentiality. For example, depending on the size of the organisation and size of the programme, is it possible to provide feedback on trends and patterns emerging from the sessions, without breaking confidentiality?
- *Issues*: Challenges and difficulties the organisation may foresee regarding the programme.
- *Escalating and safeguarding*: What is the safeguarding policy and who is the point of contact should issues that need to be escalated emerge, such as bullying, radicalisation, sexual exploitation, and self-harm?
- *Evaluation*: This needs to be scoped with the sponsor and aligned with the needs the programme is being designed to meet. Some organisations will have their established evaluation methodologies while others may need your support in choosing suitable evaluation tools. If you work with the not-for-profit sector, the evaluation may need to be aligned with the requirements laid out by the funders.
- *Commercial contract*: What are the cancellation policy, terms of payment, breach of contract conditions, professional conduct/code of ethics, complaints procedure, intellectual property (if you create materials for the programme) and termination?

7.2 Group coaching guidelines

- *Group size*: Group coaching takes place in small groups of up to 10 clients. There are no studies into participant numbers in either group or team coaching. In my professional experience, groups of between eight and 10 participants work best because they give participants the opportunity to interact with each other more meaningfully than larger groups. It also means that, if people drop out or cannot attend a session, you still have a group of a workable size.

- *Theme*: Group coaching programmes work better when they have a focused theme that is of interest to all clients. In communities and organisations, these themes will be decided according to the clients' needs and desired outcomes.
- *Length/frequency of sessions*: The periodicity varies according to the purpose of the coaching as well as the framework used. Sessions can be delivered weekly, fortnightly or monthly. It is important to consider the demographic and context. Work closely with those commissioning the coaching to understand the clients you will be coaching, including the incentives and barriers for them to participate and engage with the programme.
- *Format*: Sessions can be delivered face-to-face or virtually; a group coaching programme typically includes a number of sessions over a defined period.
- *Coach*: The coach should be trained and supervised in group work (Ward, 2008) in order to be able to tap into a range of coaching principles and models, according to their professional expertise.
- *Goals/outcomes*: The goals and outcomes for the coaching programme are defined by each client. Yalom (1995) describes how the 'nature of the relationships between the parties involved' in the group can shift their attention from the 'what' to the 'how' (p. 250). In other words, while the content and achieving goals may be important to group progress, it is even more important for group members to focus on the process of participation and learning together. With that said, because group coaching relies on the participants immersing themselves in the experience of being in the group and communicating with each other, some authors have called for group coaches to be well versed in group dynamics (Brown & Grant, 2010).
- *Process*: Coaches may use various tools and techniques. The sessions involve creating a safe space for group members to interact with each other. The coach coaches the group simultaneously.

Tips for success

1 Take time to contract well at the beginning of the programme; remember that each group will have their own needs and therefore you will need to adapt your approach to contracting to meet these needs. Be prepared to re-contract if necessary.
2 Work hard at the beginning of the group process to establish the group.
3 If the group is working well, let the group do the work. Hold the space, not the limelight.
4 Give everyone a choice as to how they interact with and contribute to the group. Avoid putting people on the spot.
5 Encourage collective and personal accountability.
6 Be aware of the cultural diversity and intersecting identities in your group, and understand the impact of your own identity.
7 Enjoy the work!

Virtual delivery

Virtual groups can work well. They are particularly effective for people who are not able to travel or are housebound. And, for organisations, virtual groups can bring together employees based in various locations, which can be particularly helpful for cross-fertilisation of ideas and for sharing perspectives and challenges.

For example, I recently worked with a group of managers from a multinational organisation. The aim of the programme was to support them to reflect on and implement best practice to support employees' wellbeing. The organisation was concerned about its retention rates after the pandemic and, although the numbers varied across countries, due to particular socio-economic circumstances affecting the job market, they believed there was room for improvement across the board. The group coaching programme was part of an engagement initiative to inform the wellbeing strategy going forward. The feedback was overwhelmingly positive, with the following highlights:

- Better understanding of the challenges facing other parts of the organisations
- Recognition of what is already working for some and discussions about how to share these examples with others more effectively.

Practical considerations of virtual group coaching

Despite the benefits of virtual groups, there are challenges and considerations for coaches to think about. The challenges are mainly linked to group dynamics, our ability to read the body language of participants, and the fact that we cannot make eye contact with participants. On the other hand, you may notice facial expressions more acutely, even tiny fleeting ones. The same applies to your own facial expressions, which may be more noticeable to clients. You are also able to see everyone at the same time, including yourself – although, in some platforms, you can choose to remove yourself from view, if you wish.

Here are some points to note when doing virtual group coaching:

- *Cameras*: Given the importance of interactions and trust for groups to work well, members must agree to have their cameras on at all times. Having group members with their cameras off can have an adverse impact on the group and other members. In the groups I have worked with, clients have raised concerns about confidentiality; if someone has their camera and mic off, some people felt unsafe to share freely. At the end of the day, for groups to work, members need to feel comfortable and engaged. That said, some coaches have different opinions about this and do not demand that everyone is on camera at all times; you need to decide what feels comfortable for you and the clients you are working with.
- *Electronic hand*: I do not ask group members to use the electronic hand. I am in favour of encouraging spontaneous interactions among group members and find that, even if people talk over each other to start with, they soon find a rhythm and a way to negotiate turns. Having the cameras on helps people read the body language of when people are ready to talk.

- *Dress code*: I never thought about adding this to my contracting in groups until I had a member join a group wearing just a dressing gown! Since then, this is on the coaching agreement I send to people before the programme starts.
- *Presence*: Discuss with the client the importance of being fully present and avoiding distractions as much as possible.
- *Confidentiality*: Having the cameras on at all times ensures that group members can see each other's environment; encourage the use of headphones if other people are able to hear the conversation and ask people to avoid being interrupted by others. Of course, we understand that sometimes these interruptions may be unavoidable and out of our control.
- *Chat function*: You have to decide whether this will be active or not, as it can be distracting and difficult to follow a live conversation and the chat at the same time. However, depending on the client group, the chat may help to get people engaged.
- *Eating and drinking*: Are people allowed to eat and drink during the session? Whereas sipping tea or water may not interfere with the flow of the session, someone munching on biscuits or eating a full lunch may. Consider the type of group you are running and use your discretion when deciding about this.
- *Body language*: Remember that, because the frame of the camera is limited to the upper part of your body with a focus on your face, even slight expressions and smaller movements can be noticed, all of which can impact on group dynamics. As a coach, unlike face-to-face interactions, you are able to look at all participants at once and you also may want to consider whether you include yourself in the frame or not (this is not possible on all virtual platforms).

8 The future of coaching for wellbeing

Wellbeing is a rewarding field of coaching, which continues to expand as individuals, communities and organisations understand the value it brings to individuals' sense of being well and the positive impact this has in various areas of their lives.

There seems to be a recognition that life as it is, in the twenty-first century in Western society, is simply not sustainable. It is not a coincidence that wellbeing, as a concept, has climbed up the agenda. After a long time of encouraging 'human doings', which unfortunately is still a condition of contemporary society, we need to get back to basics and nurture our 'being'.

The 'happiness revolution' was, according to Layard and Ward (2020), facilitated by secular ethics and enabled by the development of the science of happiness and 'of mind-training which enables us all to get a better control over our inner mental life' (p. 4). The happiness movement has certainly evolved to encompass all things related to wellbeing as well as other approaches adopted to help people flourish, coaching being one of them. It moved from a focus on the happiness-hedonic paradigm to a vision of wellbeing which encompasses both hedonic and eudaimonic philosophies. This is reflected in the field of positive psychology, where the second wave, which embraces the whole spectrum of human experience, came in to balance the notion that positive psychology was leaning towards toxic positivity (Ehrenreich, 2010).

The hedonic and eudaimonic philosophies invite us to contemplate what it takes to create a good life; they also give us insights into perspectives on being well and feeling good while acknowledging the rich tapestry of life in its totality, not only the positive side of it. In Western societies, we seem to have a 'culture of deficit'; by that, I mean we tend to focus on the gaps, on what is missing, on what we don't have. On top of that, we have the discourse of success, performance, growth and achievement. Never a moment to rest, and we are off to the next challenge, and then the next – *ad infinitum*. This culture is taking its toll, in families, workplaces, schools. It is affecting our children and adolescents. Unless we stop to take stock and make an effort to live with intention, we can easily live on autopilot. The issue with that is that we may not recognise what is damaging our wellbeing or, if we do recognise it, we may feel powerless to do anything about it. We may also miss the things that nurture us because we are too busy to appreciate and savour them.

As coaching for wellbeing continues to evolve, our understanding of the topic expands beyond the hedonic/eudaimonic dichotomy to include societal factors that are outside each individual's subjective experience and their sphere of control, but which have a direct impact on their wellbeing. As coaches, we need to be mindful of the tightrope between individual choice and self-determination and systemic issues, and our professional responsibility.

In coaching, it is crucial to develop an understanding of the limitations of the work that we do and its place within the system. And, as we take coaching for wellbeing to more people in organisations and communities, including a wide range of settings, such as schools, care homes, community groups, and patient groups, to name just a few, we must do so with professionalism and awareness of the choices we make, the approaches we use, and the research and evidence informing these approaches. This book has given you an overview of the theoretical foundations of wellbeing and coaching for wellbeing, and shared some of the evidence available to support our practice. Consider it a roadmap, and there is a lot more that you could explore and learn, should you wish to do so.

The BeWell Coaching for Wellbeing model

As an example of how theories and evidence can be applied, the book has also explained the BeWell model and its application in detail. The model has three parts – Be, Relate and Act. The first part (Be) helps clients achieve clarity around their values, purpose and meaning. The second part (Relate) includes a 'sense of belonging' and 'feeling connected'. Act is the third part of the model, and it includes wellbeing goals/outcomes and accomplishments. This empirically-tested multi-theoretical model links the theory and practice of coaching for wellbeing by bringing together hedonic and eudaimonic concepts, in the form of psychological wellbeing theory and positive psychology, alongside cognitive behavioural principles and coaching tools to support sustainable change.

Future prospects

Idealistically, I would like to see coaching for wellbeing available to as many people as possible, in as many settings as possible, not only those who need extra support to flourish, but also as a preventative intervention for individuals of all ages and backgrounds.

According to the World Health Organization (2022), mental health conditions are highly prevalent in all countries, with one in eight people in the world living with a mental disorder. Anxiety and depressive disorders are the most common. The exact cause of most mental illnesses is not known, but research points to a combination of contributing factors: genetic, biological, psychological and environmental. Figures can be even higher among people living in socio-economic deprivation; those who experience social exclusion and stigma, such as the homeless; asylum seekers and minority communities; people who live with long-term physical health conditions; carers; and those with a history of substance abuse.

Coaching for wellbeing is no panacea, and, certainly, it is no substitute for psychological care for those experiencing mental illness. It could, however, be more widely used to help people increase their understanding of wellbeing and explore ways to improve it. For organisations committed to supporting the wellbeing of employees, coaching – both individual and in groups – can be effectively and efficiently used as part of their wellbeing strategy.

You: the wellbeing coach

Having got to the end of this book, I hope it has helped you reflect on your own wellbeing and inspired you to create your own wellbeing vision. I have offered you a wide range of perspectives on wellbeing and the practice of coaching in this evolving field. Perhaps you were challenged by some of the views I presented, or you felt excited to discover that your thoughts and anecdotal experience are aligned to existing research findings. Wherever your journey will take you next, I hope it will bring fulfilment and joy to you, and those you work with.

Appendix: The Wellbeing Coach's Toolkit

The wheel of wellbeing

This wheel has six segments (Figure A.1): mind, body, meaning & purpose, relationships, emotions, and environment. Ask your client to score their current experience of each of these areas from 0 to 10 with 0 being a very poor experience and 10 being a fantastic experience. Remind the client that this is just a snapshot of their experience in a particular moment in time, which can inform their choices going forward. Once the exercise is complete, the coach asks the clients which area(s) they would like to improve.

It is important not to assume that areas with low scores are the areas the client wants to focus on. The client may, in fact, decide to improve their experience in areas in the mid-range so that they create a more satisfying experience in these areas. There are also contextual and personal circumstances that may contribute to a low score in particular areas.

- *Mind*: Intellectual stimulation, learning, feeling engaged with life, focus.
- *Body*: Physical health, vitality, exercise, sleep, nutrition, relaxation.
- *Meaning & purpose*: Feeling connected to values, finding meaning in life and living with purpose and intention.
- *Emotions*: Experience a range of emotions, able to cope with negative events, kind to self, engaged in activities that bring joy/positive emotions.
- *Environment*: Pleasant physical environment at home and work, and the wider community.
- *Relationships*: Connections to others, including family, romantic relationships, and friendship groups.

The personal wheel of wellbeing

Instead of giving the client a wheel with pre-determined segments, the coach coaches the clients on all the various aspects of their lives that contribute to their wellbeing. They can make an extensive list, and the items can be clustered into themes. Ask them to choose the most important aspects and use them for their personal wheel of wellbeing (Figure A.2). Plot these areas onto the wheel and ask the client to score themselves in each of these areas. Once the exercise is complete, the coach asks the clients which area (s) they would like to improve.

The wheel of wellbeing can be a practical visual tool for the client and a reminder of the key areas of wellbeing. It can be used as a benchmark and to assess changes during the coaching programme.

Figure A.1 The wheel of wellbeing

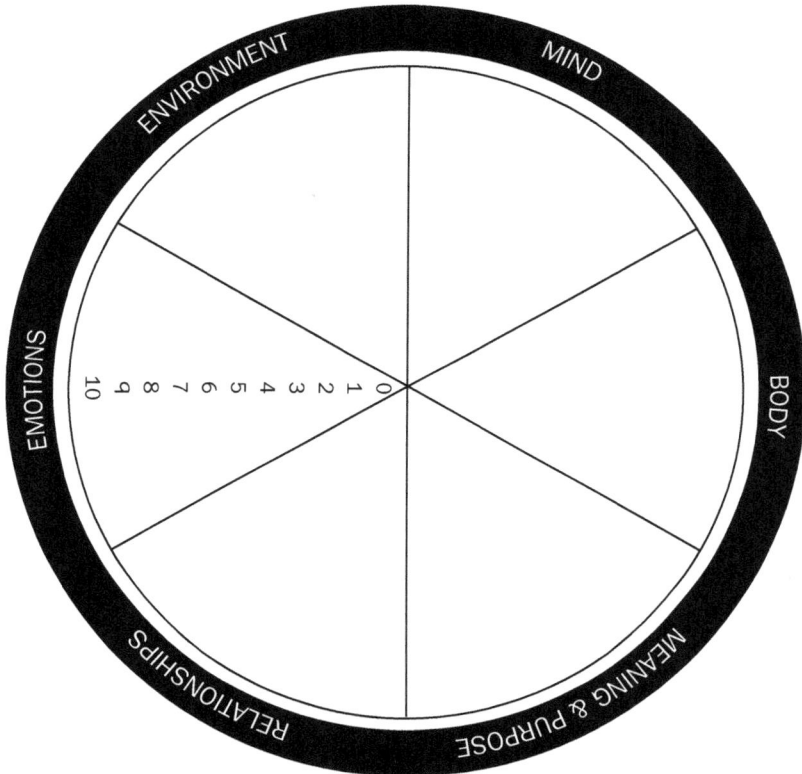

Wellbeing vision

A wellbeing vision is a representation of the client's aspirations of where they would like to be in all the several aspects of their wellbeing. It should be inspiring and exciting so that it serves as a motivator for clients. It includes all the different areas that are important for the client's wellbeing.

The client can choose how to represent their vision, for example:

- *Wellbeing vision board*: A collage of images, quotes and anything that represents the client's desired wellbeing state.
- *Wellbeing vision statement*: Written in the present tense, it includes a positive and clear summary of the client's experience of their ideal state of wellbeing.
- *Wellbeing story*: A lengthier version of the statement, it is a detailed story of the client's experience of wellbeing in various aspects of their lives.

Figure A.2 Blank wheel of wellbeing

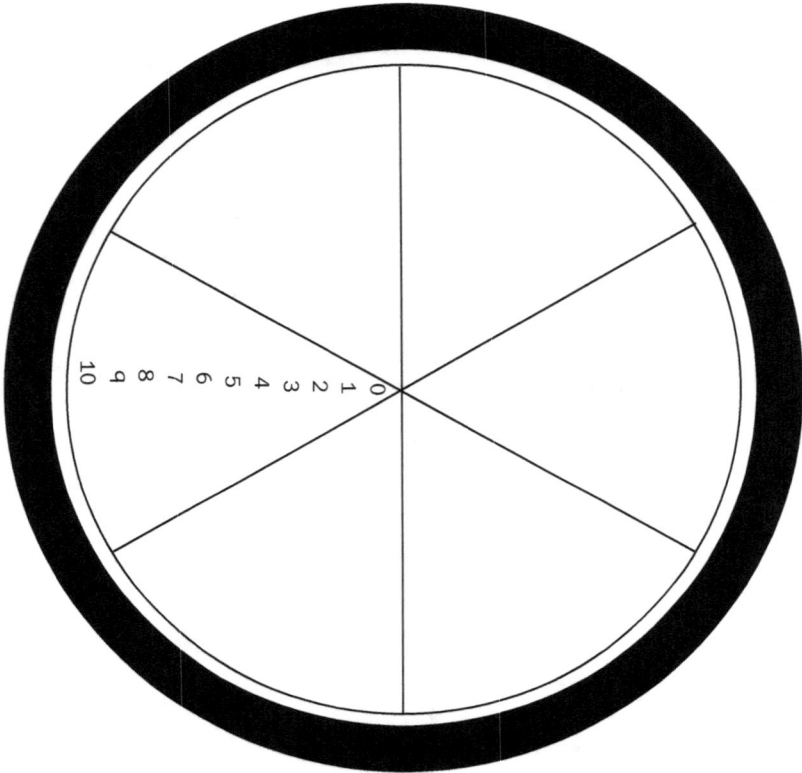

Questions to ask your client:

What is compelling about this vision? What is the most important part of this
   vision?
What will you gain from working towards this vision?
What will your life be like when you achieve your vision? How will you feel?
Who is part of your wellbeing vision?
Who can support you in achieving this vision?
What do you need to get started? What do you need to keep going?
What strengths do you already have that can help you on your way?
What are the things you need to let go?

Life story: writing your past, present and future

Writing a story about your experiences of wellbeing can help you reconnect
with memories, subjective experiences and motivations for change. It will
allow you to organise your thoughts and use them to grow.

The past

Write the story of your past in the box. Be sure to include the challenges you have overcome, and the personal strengths that allowed you to do so.

```
┌─────────────────────────────────────────────────────────────────────┐
│                                                                     │
│                                                                     │
│                                                                     │
│                                                                     │
│                                                                     │
└─────────────────────────────────────────────────────────────────────┘
```

The present

Describe your life and who you are now in the box. How are you experiencing your wellbeing at the moment? What are your strengths and what challenges are you facing? What is already in place and/or supportive of your wellbeing?

```
┌─────────────────────────────────────────────────────────────────────┐
│                                                                     │
│                                                                     │
│                                                                     │
│                                                                     │
│                                                                     │
└─────────────────────────────────────────────────────────────────────┘
```

The future

Write about your ideal future (wellbeing vision) in the box. How will your life be different from what it is now? How will you feel about yourself? What will your experiences be like?

```
┌─────────────────────────────────────────────────────────────────────┐
│                                                                     │
│                                                                     │
│                                                                     │
│                                                                     │
└─────────────────────────────────────────────────────────────────────┘
```

Values

Identifying personal values

Values reflect what is truly important to us. They serve as a compass for our life decisions. In terms of our wellbeing, we are more likely to achieve goals which are aligned to our values. Sometimes our values are clear, sometimes it requires time and reflection to help us delve into the essence of ourselves and what is genuinely significant to us, outside of societal and other external pressures. Becoming aware of your values will help you develop your goals, your choices and decisions, and recognise how much time and effort to devote to different parts of your life.

Table A.1 is a list to get you started. It is not exhaustive and you can add your own words to it. Take a moment to consider each value and its importance to you personally. Ask yourself which ones are especially important, important,

Table A.1 List of values

accomplishment	fairness	personal growth
accuracy	fame	personal responsibility
achievement	fast pace	pioneering
achieving potential	forward movement	positivity
acknowledgement	freedom	power pressure
adventure	friendship	privacy
aesthetics	fun	recognition
altruism	generosity	respect
appreciation	hard work	responsibility
artistic endeavour	harmony	results
authenticity	helping others	risk-taking
autonomy	honesty	romance
balance	humour	routine
beauty	imagination	safety
being a catalyst	independence	security
being in the flow	influencing	self-care
being my best	integrity	self-discipline
belonging	intellectual rigour	self-expression
challenge	intimacy	sensitivity
clarity	intuition	sensuality
commitment	joy	service
compassion	justice	solitude
completion	keeping promises	spirituality
connectedness	leadership	stability
contribution	learning	status
co-operation	leisure time	success
creativity	love	support
dependability	loyalty	tact
directness	making a difference	teaching
ease	making decisions	teamwork
elegance	money	tenacity
emotional health	my faith	thrill
empathy	nurturing	tolerance
empowerment	openness	tradition
encouraging	order	trust
energy	organisation	variety
entertaining	nature	vitality
environment	partnership	wealth
equality	passion	wellness
equity	peace	winning
excellence	peace of mind	wisdom
excitement	perseverance	
expertise		

quite important, and not important in your life. Similar values can be clustered and then given a name that sits well with you.

Once you have a long list of values that are meaningful to you, place a star next to the values that are 'very important' to you. Work through them until you have a short list of only five top values.

Focus on your personal values and be mindful of the values that you feel you 'ought to' have and which may be important to other people, more than to you. There may also be values which you 'would like to have' but, deep down, you know they are not as important to you.

My top five values are:

1 _____

2 _____

3 _____

4 _____

5 _____

Values questions

1 What have you learned about yourself by doing this exercise?

2 Are you living according to your values?

3 Is there anything else you would like to do to honour your values?

4 Are your wellbeing goals aligned to your values?

Cognitive distortions or unhelpful thinking patterns

These are unhelpful thinking patterns that distort our perception of reality and how we experience events in our lives. They are common and can be so habitual that people may not notice them or their impact on daily life. Below are some examples.

- *All-or-nothing thinking*: This is an either/or type of thinking with no middle ground or compromise. For example, I got one of the answers wrong so I'm a failure.
- *Personalisation*: When the person sees themselves as responsible for events around them, even the events completely outside their control. Conversely, they can place the blame on other people for events that happen in their lives.
- *Should statements*: People whose thoughts revolve around *should, ought to* and *must have*, which leads them to feel guilty and place the blame on themselves for daily events.
- *Catastrophising*: When someone goes straight to the worst-case scenario, blowing things out of proportion. The opposite phenomenon is *minimising*, when the importance of events or facts is reduced disproportionately.

- *Mind-reading*: People who make assumptions about others' feelings and behaviours without any evidence or facts to substantiate these assumptions.
- *Fortune-telling*: People who tend to predict the outcome of an event or situation, usually with a bias towards a negative outcome (they *know* that things won't turn out as expected).
- *Overgeneralisation*: People who overgeneralise often use statements including words such as 'always', 'never', 'every' or 'all'. They tend to be too broad in the conclusions they draw.
- *Discounting the positive*: Type of mental filter that discounts the positive, such as positive feedback, events and comments, by focusing only on the negative.
- *Emotional reasoning*: Mistaking one's feelings for reality is emotional reasoning. If this type of thinker feels scared, there must be a real danger.

Applying a cognitive behavioural approach

When working with clients who experience unhelpful thinking patterns and/or unhelpful thoughts, behaviours and emotions, you can use Table A.2 to explore.

Table A.2 Applying a cognitive behavioural approach

Thoughts	Emotions	Behaviour
Observe your thoughts	Emotions are information	Take a step back so you make a choice (respond as opposed to react)
Your thoughts are not facts	Notice them	Use the behaviour to trigger emotions you want
Your thoughts lead to feelings	Emotions are something we experience (not who we are)	Be accountable
Be aware of negative/ critical/emotionally draining self-talk	Notice all emotions	Choose your behaviours according to your values and aspirations
Notice where your mind goes and bring it back to the present (to make effective choices)	Practise self-regulation	
What are the alternative perspectives?		

Using Socratic questioning to challenge unhelpful thinking patterns

Socratic questioning is a method used to expose unhelpful beliefs and inconsistencies in our thinking, while considering the consequences of holding a particular view. This method is similar to coaching as it uses open-ended questions that explore 'what?', 'how?', 'who?' and 'when?'. It actively searches for different perspectives; it is driven by curiosity; and it seeks to uncover thinking, views and assumptions that are unhelpful for the client.

It is used to expose false beliefs and question what we think we know. It works like this:

- Define the basic concepts on which a belief is based.
- Expose inconsistencies.
- Highlight the consequences of holding a particular view (helpful/unhelpful).
- Then, the coach asks several questions to reveal the client's position (Table A.3).

The client can fill in Table A.4 when they have considered the questions in Table A.3.

Table A.3 Probing questions

Clarification	Explore reasons and evidence	Probe assumptions	Implications/ consequences
What makes you say that?	What would be an example?	Can you explain how you arrived at that assumption?	How does that affect...?
What do you mean by that?	What led you to believe that?	What could we assume instead?	What is important about...?

Table A.4 Challenging perceptions and thoughts

	Automatic thought	Emotion	Evidence that supports this thought	Evidence that DOES NOT support this thought	Potential alternative ways of thinking/ perspectives
Situation Event					
Situation Event					
Situation Event					
Situation Event					

Wellbeing plan

The client can fill in the wellbeing plan.

My compelling reasons to improve my wellbeing are:

1 _____

2 _____

3 _____

The client's wellbeing vision chart is shown in Table A.5.

Table A.5 Wellbeing vision chart

Things I'm already doing to support my wellbeing		
Things I want to continue doing	Things I want to start doing	Things I want to stop or say 'no' to
Things I want to do every day	Things I want to do every week	Things I want to do every month

Table A.6 Ten ways of being compassionate or critical of yourself

Not compassionate/not kind	Compassionate/kind
1	1
2	2
3	3
4	4
5	5
6	6
7	7
8	8
9	9
10	10

Self-acceptance, self-compassion and kindness

Write down 10 ways you *criticise* yourself or are *not* currently being very loving to yourself (Table A.6). Then, go back through your list, consider each point and write down what you would say or do if you were totally *compassionate and kind* to yourself.

What would help you to remind yourself to be more compassionate and kind to yourself?

Self-compassion

Be your own best friend

Self-compassion and kindness are important to our wellbeing. Sometimes our internal dialogue can be negative and overly critical, which is unhelpful and disheartening. When you notice this happening, ask yourself: 'If you said the same things to your best friend, would they still be your best friend?' If the answer is no, then think about what words you would like to say to them. Some of us find it easier to be kinder to others than to ourselves. Be your own best friend as much as possible.

Self-compassion journal

Kristin Neff (www.self-compassion.org) suggests that we write a self-compassion journal for one week to record events we feel bad about, and/or any time that we hear our self-critical voice. To write the journal, we can use mindfulness, common humanity and kindness to look at the event from a more self-compassionate way. Mindfulness is about exploring our emotions as non-judgementally as possible. Common humanity is about remembering that we are all humans; we will make mistakes; we will do things we are not proud of and we deserve to be loved with compassion for who we are, warts and all. Self-kindness is giving ourselves the same warmth and care we would give to others. This exercise helps us see our experiences using a self-compassionate perspective.

Expressive writing for wellbeing

Expressive writing can help us improve our mental, physical and emotional wellbeing (Pennebaker, 2012). Writing helps us to make sense of, explore and change our experiences. We can write the past, the present and the future; we can write like the person we want to be. We can use writing to create a vision or to work out a plan, to think about how to mitigate challenges, and find solace when things go wrong. Reflection facilitates self-awareness, and writing is a terrific way to encourage this. People have different preferences when it comes to writing. Some have a specific writing ritual; they love the feel and smell of real paper, and the process of slow writing, which gives us a sense of space and time to be. Other clients prefer writing on electronic devices – whatever works for them. I encourage my coaching clients to take notes, to write, and to explore in different forms but, if they can, to keep a record of their wellbeing journey.

How to get started

- Decide whether you will be using a notebook or an electronic device.
- Give yourself space and time for the writing; it doesn't need to be long; 10–15 mins is sufficient if you haven't got much time.
- Don't worry about the structure of your writing, spelling, punctuation or coherence – put pen to paper and just write (unfiltered if possible).
- Write about anything that is on your mind. If the process is making you distressed or upset, stop and seek further help if necessary. Writing about upsetting and traumatic things can have an adverse impact.

What should I write?

The world is your oyster when it comes to writing for wellbeing. Here are just a few suggestions:

- Positive experiences
- Gratitude notes

- Your strengths (and experiences of them)
- Recount experiences you really enjoyed
- Write to your future self about your experiences of wellbeing.

Gratitude

Three good things

At the end of each day, look back at the events of your day; write down three good things that happened; reflect on why these events went well. Do this for at least one week or keep going for as long as you like. Remember that any three good things that happened in your day will count, however small they seem to be.

Gratitude letter

Think about someone who helped you in the past and/or had a positive impact on your life and whom you have not yet thanked properly. Write that person a letter explaining how they contributed to your life and thanking them for what they did. The letter does not need to be long, but remember to be specific about what they did and the impact it has had on you, and what it has meant in your life. You decide whether to send the letter or not. If the answer is yes, you can deliver it in person, via post or email, whichever feels more appropriate. You can write as many letters as you like.

Note: both exercises were originally devised by Seligman (2012). The original gratitude letter exercise suggested, if possible and appropriate, that the letter should be delivered in person, read to the recipient and the content discussed.

Strengths

Reflect on your life experience and identify your top five strengths.

What are they? How do you use them in your life? How do your top strengths provide support? Consider how they help you with any of the following:

Your professional life
Your social life
Your relationships
Your hobbies and leisure
Your learning
Your creativity

Your strengths and your wellbeing

How can you use your strengths to support your wellbeing? Write your options in the box.

```

```

Other options for working with strengths are using the VIA Survey of Character Strengths, which I explained in Chapter 3, or use the Clifton Strengths Assessment. Its results show the individual's combination of 34 Clifton Strengths themes under four domains (strategic thinking, relationship building, influencing and executing).

Savouring

The present

If you have ever walked with a toddler, you have experienced walking with someone who notices details you never knew existed, like the texture of the pavement or colours in specks of sand; they also want to stop at every amazing new thing they come across, to explore and enjoy. Children are brilliant at living in the moment and they are curious about their environment.

To connect to our sense of wonder, and savour our present moment, a very good strategy is to use our senses. At any given time, we are partly, if not totally, oblivious to what is going on in our environment. We constantly filter information and sensations and, if we are preoccupied or focusing on our thoughts, we are less likely to notice and appreciate our experience. Here are some strategies you can use to help you fully experience the present moment and notice sounds, smells and sensations, and what you see in a lot more detail:

How many different sounds can you hear? Try to 'really' hear these sounds with your whole body.
What are the physical sensations you are experiencing in any given moment? For example, if you are out walking the dog, what is it like to feel the wind on your face? What is the temperature like? What sensations do you experience with your hands, legs, feet, etc.?

What do you see? Look out of a window and look outside as if for the first time. What do you notice now that you didn't notice before? What are the colours, the shapes and elements of the detailed landscape you are observing?

You can add savouring to your daily life by intentionally noticing specific daily events, such as going for a walk, cooking, being with loved ones, having a bath. Take a deep breath, reset and notice with your senses.

Past event

Think about a positive event, experience or moment in the past. Spend some time connecting with that moment: What is happening? Who is there? What are your thoughts? What are your feelings? What is good about that moment? What sounds do you hear? What does it feel like in your body to be experiencing that moment? Once you have reconnected fully with that experience, write it down in as much detail as possible.

Note: Bryant and Veroff's (2017) book is a good source of information if you want to expand your repertoire of savouring activities.

Meaning

Throughout this book, I have explored meaning as illustrated in theories of wellbeing along with some of its applications in coaching. Meaning in life can be seen as profound, linked to our calling in life, and anchored in our sense of self. It can also be derived from our daily lives, in other words, our 'quotidian experience' (King et al., 2016).

These distinct perspectives are important and helpful for clients and coaches to bear in mind. For some people, the very concept of 'meaning of life' can be challenging and even unattainable, while others are able to find or attribute meaning to various aspects of their lives. If the client is resistant or not ready to explore this topic, then there are plenty of other wellbeing factors from which we can choose.

A useful model to use is PURE (Wong et al., 2021), which is a framework for individuals to discover and create meanings for their lives, either by themselves or with the help of the coach.

You can help your client explore the four parts of the framework. If they want, they can then use the insights to write things down and/or create a representation of their meaning in other forms such as poetry, music, art, collage, or any other medium of their choice:

1 **P**: Purpose and life goals; what really matters in your life, your values and aspirations.
2 **U**: Understanding yourself, your drivers, beliefs and interactions in the world.

3 **R**: Responsibility and choice; acting in line with your purpose and values; doing the right thing.

4 **E**: Enjoyment/evaluating, reflecting on satisfaction with life, on how you are living your life and what you can do to improve your wellbeing.

Group coaching checklist

Programme structure

• What is the length of the programme and the number of sessions?
• What size is your group? Although this may vary, coaching groups tend to have between 6 and 10 participants maximum.
• What are the frequency and length of the sessions? (The coaching theme, sponsor, if working with an organisation, and the clients' needs may influence your decision on these points.)
• What kind of accountability tools will you use (if any)?
• How will you keep clients engaged? For example, you may decide to give them suggestions of activities they can do outside of sessions and/or send them an email or message in between sessions.

Programme delivery

• Will the programme be delivered face-to-face or online? If the latter, which platform will you use?
• Are you creating a group that will have a presence outside the sessions, such as an online forum, where they can exchange ideas? Will you be facilitating this or will the group be autonomous? What are the implications?
• What technology do you need – either to deliver the coaching online or to support the group outside of the coaching sessions?
• If running face-to-face sessions, which venue are you using?

Find out about the clients' needs, such as disabilities and/or specific requirements. When working in community settings, it is useful to ask about language barriers. You may need to adapt your materials for non-English-speaking clients and those who may find it difficult to read/write.

Getting clients on board

Regardless of whether you are recruiting people for an open group coaching for wellbeing programme or within/on behalf of an organisation, these are the things you need to consider:

• What is the overall offer of the group coaching programme? Are there any specific themes that will be addressed?

- Who will be most suited to join the group coaching programme? Any there any exclusion criteria?
- How will you recruit them? Do you have a recruitment/marketing plan?
- What information do you need to create that explains the group-coaching offer to potential clients?

If clients will be recruited by the organisation

- What is their background – age, gender, job role?
- Who is responsible for the communication with the client?
- How will GDPR issues (data protection) be handled?
- Will the organisation share your contact details with clients?
- Will you share attendance figures with the sponsor?

Contracting

Contracting is crucial in coaching and group coaching is no different. The approach you will take to contracting may depend on whether you are delivering an independent group coaching programme or the programme is delivered for, or on behalf of, an organisation. Below are some tips for effective contracting. These are in addition to the contracting you will be doing verbally with the group during the first session, which will focus on key logistics, how the group will work together, expectations and ground rules.

Independent group coaching programme guidelines

A written agreement should be sent to clients for them to sign/agree to before the start of the programme. The agreement must cover all practical aspects of the programme, including:

- Brief explanation of the programme's theme
- Timing and frequency of sessions
- Mode of delivery: face-to-face or online, and address/links for the sessions
- Fees, including methods of payment and cancellation policy and refunds
- Attendance and punctuality, including how many sessions clients are allowed to miss before they are permanently excluded from the group.
- Brief explanation of group coaching and expectations: what clients can expect from you and the group and what you/the group will expect from them; professional boundaries, such as differences between group coaching and other group practices; confidentiality and safeguarding
- Coach's professional experience and credentials
- Coach's code of ethics and complaints process.

References

Allport, G. W. (1961). *Pattern and growth in personality*. New York: Holr, Rinehart & Winston.

Argyle, M., & Crossland, J. (1987). The dimensions of positive emotions. *British Journal of Social Psychology, 26*(2), 127–137.

Bachkirova, T., & Baker, S. (2018). Revisiting the issue of boundaries between coaching and counselling. In S. Palmer & A. Whybrow (eds) *Handbook of coaching psychology* (pp. 487–499). New York: Routledge.

Bandura, A. (1997). *Self-efficacy: The exercise of control*. New York: WH Freeman.

Bar, S. G. (2014). How personal systems coaching increases self-efficacy and well-being for Israeli single mothers. *International Journal of Evidence Based Coaching & Mentoring, 12*(2), 59–74.

Baumeister, R. F., & Leary, M. R. (1995). The need to belong: Desire for interpersonal attachments as a fundamental human motivation. *Psychological Bulletin, 117*(3), 497–529.

Beck, J. S., & Beck, A. T. (1995). *Cognitive therapy: Basics and beyond*. New York: Guilford Press.

Bein, T. H., Miller, W. R., & Boroughs, J. M. (1993). Motivational interviewing with alcohol outpatients. *Behavioural and Cognitive Psychotherapy, 21*(4), 347–356.

Bishop, L., Hemingway, A., & Crabtree, S. A. (2018). Lifestyle coaching for mental health difficulties: Scoping review. *Journal of Public Mental Health, 17*(1), 29–44.

Boccoli, G., Gastaldi, L., & Corso, M. (2022). The evolution of employee engagement: Towards a social and contextual construct for balancing individual performance and wellbeing dynamically. *International Journal of Management Reviews, 25*(1), 75–98.

Boehm, J. K., & Kubzansky, L. D. (2012). The heart's content: The association between positive psychological well-being and cardiovascular health. *Psychological Bulletin, 138*(4), 655–691.

Bolier, L., Haverman, M., Westerhof, G. J., Riper, H., Smit, F., & Bohlmeijer, E. (2013). Positive psychology interventions: A meta-analysis of randomized controlled studies. *BMC Public Health, 13*(1), 119.

Bonneywell, S. (2016). Exploring the experience of simultaneous individual and group coaching of female leaders in a multinational organisation. Oxford: Oxford Brookes University.

Boyatzis, R. E., & Howard, A. (2013). When goal setting helps and hinders sustained, desired change. In S. David & D. Clutterbuck (eds). *Beyond goals: Effective strategies for coaching and mentoring* (pp. 211–228). New York: Routledge.

Brown, S. & Grant, A. (2010). From GROW to GROUP: Theoretical issues and a practical model for group coaching in organisations. *Coaching: An International Journal of Theory, Research and Practice, 3*(1), 30–45.

Bryant, F. B., & Veroff, J. (2017). *Savoring: A new model of positive experience*. Hove: Psychology Press.

Buckley, A. (2010). Coaching and mental health. In E. Cox, T. Bachkirova, & D. Clutterbuck (Eds.), *The complete handbook of coaching*. Thousand Oaks, CA: Sage.

Bühler, C. (1935). The curve of life as studied in biographies. *Journal of Applied Psychology, 19*(4), 405–409.

Butler, A. C., Chapman, J. E., Forman, E. M., & Beck, A. T. (2006). The empirical status of cognitive-behavioral therapy: A review of meta-analyses. *Clinical Psychology Review, 26*(1), 17–31.

Byrne, U. (2005). Work-life balance: Why are we talking about it at all? *Business Information Review, 22*(1), 53–59.

Caprara, G. V., Steca, P., Gerbino, M., Paciello, M., & Vecchio, G. M. (2006). Looking for adolescents' well-being: Self-efficacy beliefs as determinants of positive thinking and happiness. *Epidemiology and Psychiatric Sciences, 15*(1), 30–43.

Carr, A., Cullen, K., Keeney, C., Canning, C., Mooney, O., Chinseallaigh, E., & O'Dowd, A. (2021). Effectiveness of positive psychology interventions: A systematic review and meta-analysis. *The Journal of Positive Psychology, 16*(6), 749–769.

Carter, A., & Mason, B. (2021). *Coaching for wellbeing: Infographic.* I. f. E. Studies. https://www.employment-studies.co.uk/resource/coaching-wellbeing-infographic

Cavanagh, M., & Buckley, A. (2014). Coaching and mental health. In E. Cox, T. Bachkirova, & D. Clutterbuck (Eds.), *The complete handbook of coaching* (pp. 405–417). Thousand Oaks, CA: Sage.

CIPD. (2021). *Health and wellbeing at work survey 2021.* London: Chartered Institute of Personnel and Development.

Clutterbuck, D., Whitaker, C., & Lucas, M. (2016). *Coaching supervision: A practical guide for supervisees.* London: Routledge.

Csikszentmihalyi, M. (1990). *Flow: The psychology of optimal experience.* New York. Harper & Row.

Davis, S. P. (2015). Coaching, well-being and organisational culture: a case study of the Executive Leadership Development Programme (EDLP) in Royal Mail (UK). Oxford: Oxford Brookes University.

De Beauvoir, S. (2010). *The second sex.* New York: Knopf.

Deci, E. L., & Ryan, R. M. (1991). A motivational approach to self: Integration in personality. In R. A. Dienstbier (ed.), *Nebraska Symposium on Motivation, 1990: Perspectives on motivation* (pp. 237–288). Lincoln, NE: University of Nebraska Press.

DiClemente, C. C., & Prochaska, J. O. (1998). Toward a comprehensive, transtheoretical model of change: Stages of change and addictive behaviors. In W. R. Miller & N. Heather (eds.), *Treating addictive behaviors* (pp. 3–24). New York: Plenum Press.

Diener, E. (1984). Subjective well-being. *Psychological Bulletin, 95*(3), 542–575.

Diener, E. (2000). Subjective well-being. The science of happiness and a proposal for a national index. *The American Psychologist, 55*(1), 34–43.

Diener, E., Emmons, R. A., Larsen, R. J., & Griffin, S. (1985). The Satisfaction With Life Scale. *Journal of Personality Assessment, 49*(1), 71–75. https://doi.org/10.1207/s15327752jpa4901_13

Diener, E., Schwarz, N., & Kahneman, D. (1999). *Well-being: The foundations of hedonic psychology.* New York: Russell Sage Foundation.

Dodge, R., Daly, A. P., Huyton, J., & Sanders, L. D. (2012). The challenge of defining wellbeing. *International Journal of Wellbeing, 2*(3), 222–235. https://doi.org/10.5502/ijw.v2.i3.4

Donaldson, S. I., & Donaldson, S. I. (2021). Examining PERMA+ 4 and work role performance beyond self-report bias: Insights from multitrait-multimethod analyses. *The Journal of Positive Psychology, 17*(6), 1–10.

Duffy, R. D., & Dik, B. J. (2013). Research on calling: What have we learned and where are we going? *Journal of Vocational Behavior, 83*(3), 428–436.

Duffy, R. D., Dik, B. J., Douglass, R. P., England, J. W., & Velez, B. L. (2018). Work as a calling: A theoretical model. *Journal of Counseling Psychology, 65*(4), 423–439.

Earnshaw, V. A., & Chaudoir, S. R. (2009). From conceptualizing to measuring HIV stigma: A review of HIV stigma mechanism measures. *AIDS and Behavior, 13*(6), 1160–1177.

Ehrenreich, B. (2010). *Smile or die: How positive thinking fooled America and the world.* Cambridge: Granta Books.

Ellis, A. (1962). *Reason and emotion in psychotherapy.* New York: Carol Publishing Group.

Emmons, R. A. (1992). Abstract versus concrete goals: Personal striving level, physical illness, and psychological well-being. *Journal of Personality and Social Psychology, 62*(2), 292–300.

Erenrich, R., Burchett, C., Seidel, L., Brennan-Ing, M., & Karpiak, S. (2019). 'There are worse things than AIDS, like loneliness': A qualitative study of social isolation and loneliness among older adults with HIV in 4 regions. APHA's 2019 Annual Meeting and Expo (2–6 November).

Erikson, E. (1959). Theory of identity development. In E. Erikson, *Identity and the life cycle.* New York: International Universities Press. http://childdevpsychology.yolasite com/resources/theory% 20of% 20ident ity% 20erikson. pdf.

Falecki, D., Leach, C., & Green, S. (2018). Positive psychology coaching in practice. In S. Green & S. Palmer (eds), *Positive psychology coaching in practice.* New York: Routledge.

Fekete, E. M., Williams, S. L., & Skinta, M. D. (2018). Internalised HIV-stigma, loneliness, depressive symptoms and sleep quality in people living with HIV. *Psychology & Health, 33*(3), 398–415.

Fordyce, M. W. (1977). Development of a program to increase personal happiness. *Journal of Counseling Psychology, 24*(6), 511–521.

Fordyce, M. W. (1983). A program to increase happiness: Further studies. *Journal of Counseling Psychology, 30*(4), 483–498.

Frankl, V. E. (1985). *Man's search for meaning.* New York: Simon & Schuster.

Frankl, V. E. (1992). *Man's search for meaning: An introduction to logotherapy* .(trans. I. Lasch), Boston: Beacon Press.

Fredrickson, B. L. (2004). The broaden-and-build theory of positive emotions. *Philosophical Transactions of the Royal Society of London. Series B, Biological Sciences, 359*(1449), 1367–1377.

Fredrickson, B. L., & Joiner, T. (2002). Positive emotions trigger upward spirals toward emotional well-being. *Psychological Science, 13*(2), 172–175.

Gable, S. L., & Haidt, J. (2005). What (and why) is positive psychology? *Review of General Psychology, 9*(2), 103–110.

Gander, F., Proyer, R. T., & Ruch, W. (2016). Positive psychology interventions addressing pleasure, engagement, meaning, positive relationships, and accomplishment increase well-being and ameliorate depressive symptoms: A randomized, placebo-controlled online study. *Frontiers in Psychology, 7*, no. 686.

Giannopoulos, V. L., & Vella-Brodrick, D. A. (2011). Effects of positive interventions and orientations to happiness on subjective well-being. *The Journal of Positive Psychology, 6*(2), 95–105.

Goldman Sachs & Co. (2021).Working Conditions Survey. London: Goldman Sachs LLC.

Grant, A. M. (2003). The impact of life coaching on goal attainment, metacognition and mental health. *Social Behavior and Personality: An International Journal, 31*(3), 253–263.

Green, L., Norrish, J., Vella-Brodrick, D., & Grant, A. (2014). Enhancing wellbeing and goal striving in senior high school students: Comparing evidence-based coaching and positive psychology interventions. www.semanticscholar.org/paper/Enhancing-well.

Griffiths, K., & Campbell, M. A. (2008). Semantics or substance? Preliminary evidence in the debate between life coaching and counselling. *Coaching: An International Journal of Theory, Research and Practice, 1*(2), 164–175.

Gyllensten, K., & Palmer, S. (2005). Can coaching reduce workplace stress? A quasi-experimental study. *International Journal of Evidence Based Coaching and Mentoring, 3*(2), 75–85.

Hill, P. L., & Turiano, N. A. (2014). Purpose in life as a predictor of mortality across adulthood. *Psychological Science, 25*(7), 1482–1486. https://doi.org/10.1177/0956797614531799

Hofmann, S. G., Asnaani, A., Vonk, I. J., Sawyer, A. T., & Fang, A. (2012). The efficacy of cognitive behavioral therapy: A review of meta-analyses. *Cognitive Therapy and Research, 36*(5), 427–440.

Huta, V. (2013). Pursuing eudaimonia versus hedonia: Distinctions, similarities, and relationships. In A. S. Waterman (ed.), *The best within us: Positive psychology perspectives on eudaimonia* (pp. 139–158). Washington, DC: American Psychological Association.

Huta, V., & Waterman, A. S. (2014). Eudaimonia and its distinction from hedonia: Developing a classification and terminology for understanding conceptual and operational definitions. *Journal of Happiness Studies, 15*(6), 1425–1456.

Isen, A. M., & Levin, P. F. (1972). Effect of feeling good on helping: Cookies and kindness. *Journal of Personality and Social Psychology, 21*(3), 384–388. https://doi.org/10.1037/h0032317

Jahoda, M. (1958). *Current concepts of positive mental health.* New York: Basic Books.

Janis, I. L., & Mann, L. (1977). *Decision making: A psychological analysis of conflict, choice, and commitment.* New York: Free Press.

Joseph, S. (2015). *Positive psychology in practice: Promoting human flourishing in work, health, education, and everyday life.* Wiley Online Library.

Joshanloo, M. (2014). Eastern conceptualizations of happiness: Fundamental differences with western views. *Journal of Happiness Studies, 15*(2), 475–493.

Jung, C. (1933). *Modern man in search of a soul.* Trans. W. S. Dell & C. F. Baynes. New York: Harcourt, Brace & World.

Kashdan, T. B., Biswas-Diener, R., & King, L. A. (2008). Reconsidering happiness: The costs of distinguishing between hedonics and eudaimonia. *The Journal of Positive Psychology, 3*(4), 219–233. https://doi.org/10.1080/17439760802303044

Kenrick, D. T., Griskevicius, V., Neuberg, S. L., & Schaller, M. (2010). Renovating the pyramid of needs: Contemporary extensions built upon ancient foundations. *Perspectives on Psychological Science, 5*(3), 292–314.

Kerns, C. M., Roux, A. M., Connell, J. E., & Shattuck, P. T. (2016). Adapting cognitive behavioral techniques to address anxiety and depression in cognitively able emerging adults on the autism spectrum. *Cognitive and Behavioral Practice, 23*(3), 329–340.

Keyes, C. (2002). The mental health continuum: From languishing to flourishing in life. *Journal of Health and Social Behavior, 43*(2), 207–222.

Kim, S. H. (2014). Evidence-based (simple but effective) advice for college students: Microaction and macrochange. *The Mentor: Innovative Scholarship on Academic Advising, 16.*

Kimsey-House, H., Kimsey-House, K., Sandahl, P., & Whitworth, L. (2010). *Co-active coaching: Changing business, transforming lives.* London: Hachette UK.

King, L. A., Heintzelman, S. J., & Ward, S. J. (2016). Beyond the search for meaning: A contemporary science of the experience of meaning in life. *Current Directions in Psychological Science, 25*(4), 211–216.

King, L. A., Hicks, J. A., Krull, J. L., & Del Gaiso, A. K. (2006). Positive affect and the experience of meaning in life. *Journal of Personality and Social Psychology, 90*(1), 179–196.

Lally, P., Van Jaarsveld, C. H., Potts, H. W., & Wardle, J. (2010). How are habits formed?: Modelling habit formation in the real world. *European Journal of Social Psychology, 40*(6), 998–1009.

Latham, G., Seijts, G., & Slocum, J. (2016). The goal setting and goal orientation labyrinth. *Organizational Dynamics, 4*(45), 271–277.

Layard, R., & Ward, G. (2020). *Can we be happier?: Evidence and ethics.* Harmondsworth: Penguin UK.

Linley, P. A., Nielsen, K. M., Gillett, R., & Biswas-Diener, R. (2010). Using signature strengths in pursuit of goals: Effects on goal progress, need satisfaction, and well-being, and implications for coaching psychologists. *International Coaching Psychology Review, 5*(1), 6–15.

Little, B. R. (1989). Personal projects analysis: Trivial pursuits, magnificent obsessions, and the search for coherence. In D. M. Buss & N. Cantor (eds) *Personality Psychology* (pp. 15–31). New York: Springer.

Locke, E. A., & Latham, G. P. (2002). Building a practically useful theory of goal setting and task motivation: A 35-year odyssey. *American Psychologist, 57*(9), 705–717.

Locke, E. A., & Latham, G. P. (2006). New directions in goal-setting theory. *Current Directions in Psychological Science, 15*(5), 265–268.

Lomas, T., Froh, J. J., Emmons, R. A., Mishra, A., & Bono, G. (2014). Gratitude interventions. In A. C. Parks & S. Schueller (eds), *The Wiley Blackwell handbook of positive psychological interventions.* Oxford: Wiley Blackwell.

Lyubomirsky, S., King, L., & Diener, E. (2005). The benefits of frequent positive affect: Does happiness lead to success? *Psychological Bulletin, 131*(6), 803–855. https://doi.org/10.1037/0033-2909.131.6.803

Martela, F., & Steger, M. F. (2016). The three meanings of meaning in life: Distinguishing coherence, purpose, and significance. *The Journal of Positive Psychology, 11*(5), 531–545.

Maslow, A. H. (1943). A theory of human motivation. *Psychological Review, 50*(4), 370–396.

Maslow, A. H. (1968). *Toward a psychology of being.* Hoboken, NJ: John Wiley& Sons.

Maslow, A. H. (1987). *Motivation and personality* (3rd ed.). Boston, MA: Addison-Wesley.

Massarik, F. (1968). The biblioscene: The explication of subtlety. *The Journal of Applied Behavioral Science, 4*(1), 129–136.

Mbokota, G., & Reid, A. (2022). The role of group coaching in developing leadership effectiveness in a business school leadership development programme. *South African Journal of Business Management, 53*(1), 1–10.

Nacif, A. P. (2021). Group coaching for wellbeing in a community context. Thesis. Oxford Brookes University.

Neff, K. D. (2011). Self-compassion, self-esteem, and well-being. *Social and Personality Psychology Compass, 5*(1), 1–12.

Neugarten, B. L. (1968). The awareness of middle age. In *Middle Age and Aging* (pp. 93–98). Chicago: University of Chicago Press.

Oades, L. G. (2015). Coaching for wellbeing at work. In C. van Nieuwerburgh (ed.), *Coaching in professional contexts.* London: Sage.

Palmer, S., & Gyllensten, K. (2008). How cognitive behavioural, rational emotive behavioural or multimodal coaching could prevent mental health problems, enhance performance and reduce work related stress. *Journal of Rational-Emotive & Cognitive-Behavior Therapy, 26*(1), 38–52.

Palmer, S., Tubbs, I., & Whybrow, A. (2003). Health coaching to facilitate the promotion of healthy behaviour and achievement of health-related goals. *International Journal of Health Promotion and Education, 41*(3), 91–93.

Passmore, J., & Oades, L. G. (2014). Positive psychology coaching: A model for coaching practice. *The Coaching Psychologist, 10*(2), 68–70.

Pega, F., Náfrádi, B., Momen, N. C., Ujita, Y., Streicher, K. N., Prüss-Üstün, A. M., . . . Fischer, F. M. (2021). Global, regional, and national burdens of ischemic heart disease and stroke attributable to exposure to long working hours for 194 countries, 2000–2016: A systematic analysis from the WHO/ILO Joint Estimates of the Work-related Burden of Disease and Injury. *Environment International, 154*, 106595.

Pennebaker, J. W. (2012). *Opening up: The healing power of expressing emotions*. New York: Guilford Press.

Peterson, C., & Seligman, M. E. (2004). *Character strengths and virtues: A handbook and classification* (vol. 1). Oxford: Oxford University Press.

Prasko, J., Mainerova, B., Jelenova, D., Kamaradova, D., & Sigmundova, Z. (2012). Existential perspectives and cognitive behavioral therapy. *Activitas Nervosa Superior Rediviva, 54*(1), 3–14.

Pressman, S. D., & Cohen, S. (2005). Does positive affect influence health? *Psychological Bulletin, 131*(6), 925–971. https://doi.org/10.1037/0033-2909.131.6.925

Rogers, C. R. (1957). The necessary and sufficient conditions of therapeutic personality change. *Journal of Consulting Psychology, 21*(2), 95–203.

Rotter, J. B. (1966). Generalized expectancies for internal versus external control of reinforcement. *Psychological Monographs: General and Applied, 80*(1), 1.

Rozin, P., & Royzman, E. B. (2001). Negativity bias, negativity dominance, and contagion. *Personality and Social Psychology review, 5*(4), 296–320.

Ryan, R. M. (2017). *Self-determination theory: Basic psychological needs in motivation, development, and wellness*. New York: Guilford Press.

Ryan, R. M., & Deci, E. L. (2000). Self-determination theory and the facilitation of intrinsic motivation, social development, and well-being. *American Psychologist, 55*(1), 68–78.

Ryan, R. M., & Deci, E. L. (2001). On happiness and human potentialS: A review of research on hedonic and eudaimonic well-being. *Annual Review of Psychology, 52*, 141–166.

Ryan, R. M., Huta, V., & Deci, E. (2008). Living well: A self-determination theory perspective on eudaimonia. *An Interdisciplinary Forum on Subjective Well-Being, 9*(1), 139–170. https://doi.org/10.1007/s10902-006-9023-4

Ryff, C. D. (1989). Happiness is everything, or is it? Explorations on the meaning of psychological well-being. *Journal of Personality and Social Psychology, 57*(6), 1069–1081. https://doi.org/10.1037/0022-3514.57.6.1069

Ryff, C. D. (2014). Psychological well-being revisited: Advances in the science and practice of eudaimonia. *Psychotherapy and Psychosomatics, 83*(1), 10–28.

Ryff, C. D., & Keyes, C. L. M. (1995). The structure of psychological well-being revisited. *Journal of Personality and Social Psychology, 69*(4), 719–727. https://doi.org/10.1037/0022-3514.69.4.719

Ryff, C. D., & Singer, B. (2008). Know thyself and become what you are: A eudaimonic approach to psychological well-being. *Journal of Happiness Studies, 9*(1), 13–39. https://doi.org/10.1007/s10902-006-9019-0

Sartre, J.-P. (1992/1943). *Being and nothingness: A phenomenological essay on ontology*. Trans. Hazel E. Barnes. London: Washington Square Press.

Seligman, M. E. (2012). *Flourish: A visionary new understanding of happiness and well-being*. New York: Simon & Schuster.

Seligman, M. E. (2018). PERMA and the building blocks of well-being. *The Journal of Positive Psychology, 13*(4), 333–335.

Seligman, M. E., & Csikszentmihalyi, M. (2000). Positive psychology. An introduction. *American Psychologist, 55*(1), 5–14.

Seligman, M. E., Steen, T. A., Park, N., & Peterson, C. (2005). Positive psychology progress: empirical validation of interventions. *American Psychologist, 60*(5), 410–421.

Sheldon, K. M., & Elliot, A. J. (1999). Goal striving, need satisfaction, and longitudinal well-being: the self-concordance model. *Journal of Personality and Social Psychology, 76*(3), 482–497.

Sin, N. L., & Lyubomirsky, S. (2009). Enhancing well-being and alleviating depressive symptoms with positive psychology interventions: A practice-friendly meta-analysis. *Journal of Clinical Psychology, 65*(5), 467–487.

Singer, T., & Klimecki, O. M. (2014). Empathy and compassion. *Current Biology, 24*(18), R875–R878.

Slade, M. (2010). Mental illness and well-being: the central importance of positive psychology and recovery approaches. *BMC health services research*, 10(1), 1–14.

Smith, C. L. (2017). Coaching for resilience and well-being. In T. Bachkirova, G. Spencce, & D. Drake (eds), *The Sage handbook of coaching* (pp. 346–362). London: Sage.

Smith, J. L., & Bryant, F. B. (2017). Savoring and well-being: Mapping the cognitive-emotional terrain of the happy mind. In M. D. Robinson & M. Eid (eds), *The happy mind: Cognitive contributions to well-being* (pp. 139–156). New York: Springer.

Smith, W.-A., Boniwell, I., & Green, S. (2021). *Positive psychology coaching in the workplace*. New York: Springer.

Snyder, C. R., & Lopez, S. J. (2009). *Oxford handbook of positive psychology* (2nd ed.). New York: Oxford University Press.

Snyder, C. R., Shorey, H. S., Cheavens, J., Pulvers, K. M., Adams III, V. H., & Wiklund, C. (2002). Hope and academic success in college. *Journal of Educational Psychology, 94*(4), 820–826.

Søvold, L. E., Naslund, J. A., Kousoulis, A. A., Saxena, S., Qoronfleh, M. W., Grobler, C., & Münter, L. (2021). Prioritizing the mental health and well-being of healthcare workers: An urgent global public health priority. *Frontiers in Public Health, 9,* 679397.

Spinelli, E., & Horner, C. (2008). An existential approach to coaching psychology. In S. Palmer & A. Whybrow (eds), *Handbook of coaching psychology* (pp. 118–132). New York: Routledge.

Steger, M. F. (2018). Meaning and well-being. In E. Diener, S. Oishi, & L. Tay (eds), *Handbook of well-being*. Salt Lake City, UT: DEF Publishers. DOI: nobascholar. com

Steger, M. F., Frazier, P., Oishi, S., & Kaler, M. (2006). The meaning in life questionnaire: Assessing the presence of and search for meaning in life. *Journal of Counseling Psychology, 53*(1), 80–93.

Steger, M. F., Mann, J. R., Michels, P., & Cooper, T. C. (2009). Meaning in life, anxiety, depression, and general health among smoking cessation patients. *Journal of Psychosomatic Research, 67*(4), 353–358.

Ward, G. (2008). Towards executive change: A psychodynamic group coaching model for short executive programmes. *International Journal of Evidence Based Coaching & Mentoring, 6*(1), 67–78.

Waterman, A. S. (1993). Two conceptions of happiness: Contrasts of personal expressiveness (eudaimonia) and hedonic enjoyment. *Journal of Personality and Social Psychology, 64*(4), 678–691. https://doi.org/10.1037/0022-3514.64.4.678

Weiss, L., Westerhof, G., & Bohlmeijer, E. (2016). Can we increase psychological well-being? The effects of interventions on psychological well-being: a meta-analysis of randomized controlled trials. *PLoS One, 11*(6), e0158092. https://doi.org/10.1371/journal.pone.0158092

Wong, P. T. (2011). Positive psychology 2.0: Towards a balanced interactive model of the good life. *Canadian Psychology/Psychologie Canadienne, 52*(2), 69–81.

Wong, P. T. (2014). Viktor Frankl's meaning-seeking model and positive psychology. In A, Batthyany & P. Russo-Netzer (eds), *Meaning in positive and existential psychology* (pp. 149–184). Berlin: Springer.

Wong, P. T., Mayer, C.-H., & Arslan, G. (2021). Existential positive psychology (pp2. 0) and the new science of flourishing through suffering. *Frontiers in Psychology*, 5661.

World Health Organization. (2022). *World mental health report: Transforming mental health for all: executive summary.* Geneva: WHO.

Yalom, I. D. (1995). *The theory and practice of group psychotherapy.* New York: Basic Books.

Yalom, I. D. (2020). *Existential psychotherapy.* London: Hachette UK.

Index

Page numbers in italics are figures; with 't' are tables.

www.ingramcontent.com/pod-product-compliance
Lightning Source LLC
Chambersburg PA
CBHW070347270326
41926CB00017B/4029